The Life & Times

Of Theodore P. Belafonte

The Life & Times

Of Theodore P. Belafonte

written by
Teddy Belafonte

Published by BlackGold Publishing

Edited by Noelle Brookes

First Edition: June 2019
Printed in the United States of America
Published by BlackGold Publishing
ISBN: 978-1-7337806-7-4

Dedication

For:
Quincy B. Adams Sr
Quincy Adams Jr
Portia Lee Adams
Nancy Watkins
Alice Louise Patten
Trestan Ricardo Adams

May you smile down at my hard work and
know you helped guide the way. I love
and miss you all so much.

To:
Josiah Garrick Reid Adams
Elijah Robert Castillo

May this book help produce all the toys,
video games and trips to Disney World
your heart's desire. I LOVE YOU.

&
To my mother,
VaNessa Adams –

Thank you for believing in me and supporting ALL OF MY ENDEAVORS!! A lifetime isn't long enough to repay all that you've done.

Special Thank You to Riptides Seafood 11212 Ironbridge Rd, Chester, VA. Thank you for letting me drink for cheap and write this book at your restaurant.

Intro

What's happenin'? My name is Teddy Belafonte, and if you're reading this, big shout out to you 'cause you purchased my book. Before reading this compilation of my random experiences and ramblings, I think it would help y'all better understand if I gave a quick background.

I had the kind of upbringing that when I explain it to folks who look like me, they might not be able to 100% relate, but they've definitely heard it before. And when I explain it to other people, it sounds a little Lifetime-ish. My folks split up when I was three, so I have no recollection of the two-parent household, which was fine. I don't think I missed out on anything cause my dad was always around, and for a good chunk of my life, I lived down the street from him. Easiest. Visitation. Ever.

I'm my mom's only child and my dad's youngest, so no matter who house I was at, I was the favorite. That's right, you got a winner on y'all hands.

Since I could remember, I've enjoyed writing, but not the traditional style (as I'm sure you can already tell). All through school, I was guaranteed to get an A+ on any form of writing that allowed my creativity to flourish. Now when it came to, "read this shit and tell me what the author meant by that one paragraph, and give me four pages," eehhhhh. A B- or a C would shine a light bright enough to get me through the dark forest I call the education system.

It wasn't until I got to THE Virginia State University and enrolled in a creative writing course, that I saw my potential. Shout out to my professor Dr. Willie Hobbs for being that push I needed, AND shout out to VSU for hiring an English professor who managed to spark young minds while embodying a real Florida Boy. Such a phenomenal feat.

After I finished college, I took a week off to drink and enjoy family, and went back to my lovely job developing photos at a drugstore. It was at this time a friend of mine told me I should start blogging my inner thoughts because my statuses on social media seemed to entertain people, so might as well take it a step further. So I started a blog that saw a surprising amount of success on social media. So I kept it up, while I waited tables, worked with adults with disabilities, worked at a probation office, worked at a high school, AND fell in love and had a child. Literally all of that, PLUS my experiences up to the beginning of this paragraph made me say, "I think I got a story to tell some folk." If you aren't inspired, then at the very least, I can make you laugh your ass off.

I've always had a knack for storytelling. I enjoy explaining the major and minor details along with the plot to get the audience engaged. People have appreciated it, although, I can see how I've also gotten on some folks nerves. I admittedly lack the ability to get straight to the point. You're reading this though, and this is literally a book of me telling you stories. Imagine we're sitting around a campfire telling funny stories. That's how I envisioned this book while putting it together.

For some, this is an edited version of my blog plus some unheard tales. For others, this is a whole journey into the Life of Teddy Belafonte. For a lot of my family, this is, "Woooooo, dat boy cuss like his daddy." For me, this is an opportunity to make people laugh, something I love doing. So again, shout out to you, yes you, for reading this. I love and appreciate your support, and I want you to know, this is only the beginning.

Quincy B

My father passed away in 2010, and as do most people who have lost loved ones, I'm always thinking about him. He had these three magical words that used to punk me. No matter the situation or argument, once he said, "What I say?" it was either do what he said, or the belt was coming.

Since I could remember, I was a decent swimmer. I'm not leaving a trail of hot tub jets behind me while swimming, but I'm also never in danger of drowning. I'm big, so I can float like nobody's business anyway. I don't have a vivid memory of being two or three years old, but I'm pretty sure my dad threw my ass in a pool one day and prayed for the very best. When I was about eight, I spent the summer with my dad in North Carolina, and he put me in swimming lessons. I moved pretty quickly from the baby pool to the 14 feet pool with diving boards and other hazards that eight year olds shouldn't be around.

I started off jumping from the low dive, like a damn champion, screaming out;
"BIIIRRRDDDDDMMMAAAAAANNNNNNN,"
and doing karate moves. Every day before we left the pool, my dad would ask if I was ready to jump off the high dive. And every day, I would be like "hell no nigga!" In so many words.

But he always told me that I was gonna jump off of the high dive before I went back to school. Actually, he said, "You ain't no CHUMP. You jumpin' off before you go back to ya mama, even if I have to throw ya ass off myself."

Loud and clear Pops.

So one day, we went to the pool, and I looked at the low dive. It's about five feet. It's really nothing. Add another ten feet and you have the gargantuan beast that I REFUSED to jump from all summer. It had just been taunting me all summer cause it KNEW I wasn't ready for it. Well, I guess this day I decided to boss up, and I looked at my dad with an eye of the tiger and said, "I'm ready." I got out the pool, climbed to the top of the high dive, looked down and almost pissed myself. That. Shit. WAS. HIGH!!

I looked at my dad. "I wanna get down."
"Jump."
"Please, it's too high."
"What I say?"

Dammit, there was the button.

Well, if HE wouldn't let me get down, I could override his call, and go to an employee of this lovely establishment. I looked at the lifeguard who was standing at the bottom of the ladder next to my dad and asked, "Can I get down please?"

She looked at my dad and he stared at her with a look that said, "You can get these hands too." My dad was pretty intimidating, so I'm pretty sure she pissed her trunks along with me. She looked at me and shook her head, no.

I thought to myself like... *Sis you really gonna let this man punk you just cause he looked at you sideways? I promise I ain't gon let him hurt you, LET ME DOWN!*

So I wiped the tears from my eyes (yes I cried, shut up). I took a step back. Took a deep breath. Then ran and jumped off that board doing some kind of unorthodox movement in the air, like those white women do on TV when they try to dance on morning talk shows.

Once I came up from the water, all the old ladies in the physical therapy pool started clapping, and my dad was all hype, with this Kool Aid smile on his face. He couldn't stop talking about it, the whole way home. He called every family member he could think of. If my dad never punked that lifeguard, I definitely would've never jumped off the high dive, and I'll never forget that. I guess what I'm tryna say is, cherished moments isn't just the first and middle name of a hoodrat. Moments like that last a lifetime.

I love you, Pops.

Errybody Hates Teddy

Little known fact: I lived in Nutsac, West Virginia for about nine months when I was 14. Yea it sucked, in case you were wondering. I was one of maybe twenty black people outta 600 (random number)? Just know we were rare round them parts. Anywho, obviously being black in a school full of eggshell colored folk with rosy throats you hear a lot of hateful words. You gotta know when to pick your battles though cause 3/4 of them people related, so if you fight one, they got a whole lineage waiting on ya ass.

Well, this one day I was on my way to the bus to leave and I'm listening to "Da Band" on my CD player (you feel old?). And this kid stuck his head out the window and said, "Whatcha say there nigger?" Chuckle.

See, I could've ignored him. I could've been the bigger person. But unfortunately for this guy I watched *The Wire* before school (shoutout to Moms having the HBO package in high school) and I had a thug quota I had to reach.

So I walked on the bus and saw that the driver wasn't on there, a clear sign that I had to Django his ass. I walked to the back where he was sitting. Had my classic mean mug on and said one of those cliche shit starter lines.

"That was sposed to be funny?? You got jokes huh??" And proceeded to throw excellent hands.

I'm not 100% on this m, but I'm pretty sure if you looked above my head you would've seen

First Attack. 2 Hit. 3 Hit. 4 Hit. 5 Hit. 6 Hit.

Once I stopped channeling E Honda, he sat there teary eyed and his friends all fell out in synchronized laughter. I felt bad (cause I always feel bad for shit like that, judge me) but then I had a level of goondom to maintain so I turnt round and walked to the front of the bus like a Chief Executive Officer.

Then the driver that was behind us got on the bus and interrogated me, "Why'd you beat that boy like that?!"

"He called me the N word.

"I don't care NUTHIN bout what he called you you, keep yer hands off um ya understand me?

Aaaannnnddddd here come the lynching mobs.

But to my surprise, Jethro didn't write me up. So not only did I become Dorner-feared on my bus, but I ain't even get in trouble for it. Touchdown! Throws yellow flag.

I called pops to tell him. His response, "Did you win?? THERE YA GO!!!"

Then, then I did something stupid. I told my mother.

My politically correct, law abiding ass mother.

HER response(s), "YOU DID WHAT?! Where did this happen? Who is he? Where does he live? WHERE did you hit him?! How HARD did you hit him?! HOW...MANY...TIMES... did you hit him?? How old is he?? Did you get in trouble? NO?! Well as SOON as you get to that school I want you to go to the office and tell SOMEBODY what you've done and accept whatever punishment you get, and if you get suspended I'm WHOOPIN YO ASS!!"

Et tu, Mother?

So I went school the next day, and the whole time I was thinking to myself, "What lie can I tell to make it seem like I got off and have mom thinking I told on myself??"

Well 6th period came around, and I got my story straight. Then, Satan intervened.

Intercom noise. "Umm, excuse me. Can you send Teddy to the office please? Thank you."

Really??? You couldn't hold off on that?? You sorry bastards.

So I walked to the office, hoping that what I'm thinking happened didn't really happen. But it did.

Yep, my mama called my guidance counselor.

BETRAYAL!!

Counselor said, "So your mother tells me you got into an altercation with another student on the bus yesterday."

"Yea... he made me mad so I hit him... a few times."

"You can't just hit people every time they make you mad. Who was this young man?"

"I don't know his name. He's my age though."

She handed me a yearbook and told me to look for him so she can call him down. I looked at the ninth graders. Didn't see him. But I did look pretty fast, so I looked again. Nope. Eighth grade. Hmmm. I didn't see him. But he was probably sick on ninth grade picture day. Yea, cause there's no way in hell he was in the seventh grade. I wouldn't do no shit like that.

Seventh grade. Hold up... that looked like him. Naw, naw that couldn't be him. Naw, def not... Alright, Teddy admit it. You proudly beat the shit out of a 7th grader. After judging me for 45 seconds, my counselor called the kid to the office.

7

Kid said, "I didn't mean to make him mad. My friends dared me to do it I just wanted to fit in, y'know not too many people like me." Cue sad TV *Orphan voice.*

Ugh. Really you lil bastard? You gonna make me feel and look worse than I already did? I oughta slap the shit outta yo- oh yea. That's why I'm here now.

"Since you both seem to be remorseful and your apologies seemed sincere I'm gonna keep this between us. But don't let this happen again."

So… It went better than expected. I didn't get in trouble. Me and that child became friends. Well not friends, but he ain't mess with anymore. And people didn't mess with me after that. I still don't 100% know why mom dukes made me tell. I know it was to teach me a lesson but still.

WHERE YO LOYALTIES AT MA?!

The Scooternator

While living in Nutsac, the school I went to was pretty big because it was the only junior high in the county. And there were only five black people. I'm exaggerating, maybe 25ish. And of course not everyone likes each other, but there was like an underlying brotherhood if something went down. But there's an exception for every rule.

So, I'm walking through the hallways of General Lee Junior High, and a fellow brother approaches me. Bro said, "Aye Teddy, you heard what happened to me?" "Naw, what?" "This damn redneck called me a nigger!" "WHO?!" "Such and such. Ima beat his ass after school, bruh."

"I mean, if you feel disrespected, then you gotta do what you gotta do."

So Bruh was small. Frail. But I thought he was one of those small dudes that had to fight his whole life. So I gave him the benefit of the doubt that he could handle himself since he had so much confidence.

Later on in the day, I was in class talking to my boy JB Snooze. "Aye you heard Bruh tryna fight some redneck that dropped the N bomb on him?" JB said, "Yeeeaaaa, everybody has been telling him not to do it cause he's gonna lose, but he won't listen."

9

"I don't know. Bruh sounded pretty confident."

"You ever seen the dude he wanna fight?"

"I can't put a face to the name, but I've probably seen him." "If you think he has a chance of winning, then you haven't seen dude. I'll show you on the way to lunch."

So he pointed the dude out. Listen. Just listen to me. This was the beginning of me being a conspiracy theorist. At the tender age of 14, I saw dude and I just KNEW that somewhere in 1967 Bull Connor was in a lab in Alabama with a bunch of Klan scientists working on a series of redneck cyborgs to send to the future and terrorize black folk. This dude was just huge for no damn reason. He looked like a shoulder wearing tight jeans and a tight ass white tee. And folk saying he just got that big working on a farm. Ain't that many hay bales in the state of West Virginia. AND by this time, I had been at the school for about five months. I'd seen about everybody in the school. I would have noticed somebody strolling round the building built like a Jeep. I was traumatized and shocked because one, unless Bruh has some cheat codes or a Gamebreaker or a mushroom, star, the ghost of Jack Johnson, he not winning.

Two, this corrupt ass school was housing this Klan cyborg that Bull Connor sent from the past. I'D NEVER SEEN HIM. And I wished someone from administration would admit that they kept his ass in a closet plugged up, charging for the first half of the school year and only let him out to terrorize black folk. So let's call him "The Scooternator."

The school day was over, and I was on my way to practice when I heard people calling Bruh name. So I know he fighting, but maybe they're cheering him on. When I got closer, they had the hallway doors closed. The window of the door was taller than me, so I was jumping up to look through it.

I really wanna tell y'all that Bruh was winning this fight. I would love nothing more than to tell you that Bruh defeated The Scooternator. FOR THE CULTURE. But, instead I have to tell you that every time I jumped up to look through the window, Bruh was being used to scrub the floor. I mean Scooternator is standing there, emotionless, dragging Bruh who I can now call The Artist Formally Known As RINSE (RIP). And folk were letting this go on. They'd formed a circle. RINSE was laying on the floor, looking like Frogger after he lost. And I was just screaming, "SOMEBODY THROW WATER ON HIM AND SHORT CIRCUIT HIS ASS! FIND A BIG ENOUGH MAGNET AND USE IT TO FRY HIS MOTHERBOARD!" My screams fell on deaf ears. Bull Connor won.

They suspended Scooternator and I didn't see him again. So I'm pretty sure he jumped in his vortex and went back to 1967 to get his next assignment. RINSE had all the respect from me for standing up to the cyborg. But he should've done his research. David had a stone and sling shot. Craig had a brick. We live in the mountains.

You're surrounded by weapons.

The Sperm Goon Chronicles

Sperm Goon equals bad. Ass. Children. Simple enough. I'd been against dating women with kids since I was 14. Not because I was influenced by years of barbershop talk and Rap City interviews. But by experience.

After divorcing my Auntie, my Uncle started dating again, and this one particular relationship he thought it'd be good to invite his son(my brousin) and I out with him, his girlfriend, and her kids. His girl, let's call her TripleDoubleMom, had CHILDREN!! I'm exaggerating. There were only three with her. But they were all handfuls, so mathematically speaking that's like 15 children. Her son, Firrstgrade48 (Goon in Training), was 9. Her daughter, EBTia (don't get me started), was 13. Her nephew, Eddie HimSlow (future professional idiot), was 11.

This one time we went to the park. We cooked out, played basketball, and joked around. Me and EBTia flirted innocently. It was a good time. We enjoyed ourselves. The very next week, these assholes decided to flip the script. This is how I know TripleDub had been single for a while, or kept her kids a secret because they had yet to figure out how long to wait to let their Goondom show. They had failed to calibrate their Goonometer. This was just the second time we'd been out together. We rolled up to their neighborhood, which was eerily similar to the one Denzel Washington's baby moms in Training Day. One way in, one way out. We went in the apartment, and we're chilling on the Saran wrapped couch, and EBTia tells me to come outside with her. So, we're outside, talking and flirting. Then apparently I said or did something she didn't like (still have no idea what it was), but she got in my face. Then said, "I SHOULD SLAP YOU."

"Man I ain't scared of you. Do it." Disclaimer: Theodore P Belafonte has never condoned violence against women.

She did it. Slapped Zeeeee shit outta me and ALL I DID was push her off, wasn't even hard.

"OOOOOOOOOO I'MA TELL MY AUNTIE."

So, she went in the house, calls her aunt, and her ass come around the corner looking like Warren Sapp. She said, "YOU WANT ME TO HOLD HIM DOWN? YOU WANT ME TO HOLD HIM DOWN? I SHOULD BEAT YOU MYSELF!"

Well. THAT escalated quickly. I was forced to apologize. So, then we all piled up in my Uncles truck. I played 'round with First48 and Ed, and we're gettin' along singing the Fiesta remix. Ed got an idea and looked at my cuzzo. Then hit him with the trick. "Did you know if your hand is bigger than your face you're a genius?"

I thought he heard it before. But I guess I was wrong

cause Cuzzo put his hand in front of his face, and Ed made this dude slap HIMSELF so hard that his glasses came off. He was HOT. I couldn't blame him cause if I slapped my glasses off my own face unwillingly, blood would have to spill before I could calm down.

So we go to the mall and play around n shit. Me and First48 still cooling and having fun ignoring EBTia. Then, on our way out, Ed stopped in a toy store. He was playing with one of those super bounce balls, and it bounced out the store. And he kept going with it. In the parking lot, TripleDouble noticed it, and asked if he paid for it.

"No... it bounced out the store so I thought I could have it." My uncle leaned into his ass something serious. "Boy you are damn near a teenager, that excuse would work if you were four. Actually, it wouldn't, cause that's just universally stupid. You're the person that's driving the car and watches your cousin kill someone, and get in your car and give him a ride home and claim you're innocent. You're Rae Carruth stupid."

Anyways...

Wanna know why I call T-Dub's son TheFirstgrade48?? cause I'm pretty sure this boy is either in prison right now or he's a drill rapper.

On our way home, he was all nice. Then he asked to

15

see my phone, and I told him no. You would've thought I said something bout his mama. He lunged at me, and EBTia grabbed him and told him to calm down. So when we got out the car, he looked at me dirty. I was like, "You mad?"

Then he sticks his pinky out and just looks at me. "What the hell is that supposed to mean?"

"It means SUCK MY DICK BIIIIIIITTTTCCCHHHH." *This 9-year-old just sonned the hell outta you. You can't go out like no punk no matter how young he is.*

I thought of the quickest comeback I could. "Why did you stick your pinky out then? cause it's actual size?"

OOOOOOOOOOOOOOOOOOOOHHHHHHHOOO OOOOOOOOO. GOOOOOOTTTT EEEEEEMMMMMMMM.

Then he got mad again and came at me. EBTia grabbed him again, so he started telling me that he couldn't wait to watch me die and other crazy shit like that. Then for some reason, EBTia got mad at me (Ain't nobody in this family messing with a full deck of cards. Just a household fulla SSI checks.), and she threatened to let him go and let him eat me alive. "Man I ain't scared of you. Do something."
"Bro, he said the same thing to me. Go over there. He ain't gonna do nothing. He was scared of auntie.

Teddy, I'ma let him go."
"Go ahead. But if your brother comes near me, I'm punching him in the face."

EBTia let him go. Welp. Time to introduce them to Hands Christian Andersen.

FirstGrade48 came running towards me, full speed, screaming some damn battle cry. I swung at him like I was throwing a baseball. I hit AWWLLL forehead too, left his frontal lobe swollen. He on the ground crying, and I don't know if I should feel proud that I ain't let this family ho me a second time, or disappointed in myself cause I did just fade the hell out of a nine year-old.

You can imagine after that my Uncle's date went to hell. I'm not sure if they went out again. I know that's the last time my black ass got invited to go with them. Since then, I've been against dating women with kids. Until 2013, when I met my future son's mother and his yet-to-be older brother.

Life comes at you fast, bruh.

The Rise & Fall Of Hoodrat Infatuation

So, my freshman year in college, I had this strange attraction to hoodrats. It was something sexy to me about red micro braids and hot pink skinny jeans. The Jordan's, the Daisy dukes, and the wife beater with the "she might be a lil pregnant, might be Four Loko" stomach bump. Judge me.

There was this one hoodrat I had class with that I had a skrong crush on. Let's just call her Aretha Stanklin. Eventually, I got her number, and we went out to McDonalds cause hoodrats are easily flattered (and I was broke). We were at the drive thru window, and the lady had a stank attitude. While at the window, Ms. Stanklin asked the lady for a lot of extra ketchup. The lady was rushing me, so I took the ketchup and tossed it in her lap. I didn't throw it like a pitcher with a lot of hate in my heart. I lightly tossed it. BIG MISTAKE.

"NIGGA DID YOU JUST THROW KETCHUP AT ME?!?!" "I was just playing; it's all love."

"NO NIGGA WON'T NOBODY PLAYING! HOW DARE YOU! I OUGHTA GRAB THE WHEEL AND KILL US BOTH."

"Chill, you acting like I swung at you or something. I was just playing, my bad." "NIGGA YOU GON HIT ME?! I'LL CALL AWL MY BROVAS UP TO COME BANK YOU!"

"Over ketchup??"

"NIGGA THIS IS DEEPER THAN MUHFUGGIN KETCHUP!"

I hold in a laugh.

"Just take me home, Teddy. I'm done."

Later she apologized, and we went out to the mall. On the way back, I stopped by my boy's job to pick up something and introduced him to her. On the way home, she hit the button.

"Teddy, don't be showing me off to people like I'm yo girl. We just cool, niigga." "I clearly went to my boys job to get this money from him, and I felt it rude to not introduce y'all. Don't hype yourself."
"Nigga I'm BAD. I'm off the f*ckin charts. I know what you was doing."

More statements like that followed. This one of the rare moments I started hulkin' up.

"Shut UP. You been naggin' me for three f*ckin weeks. Just SHUT yo ass UP and leave me alone."

"Teddy, you're scaring me. Just calm down." *I'm scaring her? What's a goon to a goblin?* "Stop talking cause you making it worse. Just sit back, stop talking, and let me take you home!"

19

"Ok Teddy, I'll go out with you again. Just stop."

"Are you serious?! I can't wait to get you out the car. What makes you think I wanna go out with you again?" "Nigga, I been texting my brovas everything you been telling me. They ready to F*CK you up!" *Teddy, she just bluffing, bruh.*

"Whatever girl."

Then she called 'em, and put em on speaker phone. And all I heard was, "YEA NIGGA IT'S OVER FOR YOU WHEN YOU COME BACK TO THE BURG!" and other voices in the back. Then she's like "Tell Twan to get the tool."

…the tool??

Oooohhh Teddy, we never rehearsed this. Ight, just be cool, pull ya black & mild out and light it. And keep the same mug on your face you been had. LOOK THE PART. COMMITT TO IT!

Ten minutes of silence. Then she said, "I called em off, Teddy. They not gonna do anything."

This led me to believe everything was bullshit. But you know, I'm tryna live. I sat there, sans tool, and there may or may not be a goon convention outside my dorm. If there was ONE dude who was a student , I wouldn't even be concerned. But her brothers were locals, who had nothing to lose, and probably treated shooting somebody like a Bar Mitzvah. And you know what? I ain't ashamed to say it. Her scare tactics worked. Ms Stanklin-1. Teddy-0.

Ain't seen her since.
Maybe this hoodrat infatuation wasn't healthy.

Might Don't Make It

My name is Teddy Belafonte, and I am admittedly hardheaded. I still eat cheesecake knowing I'm very much so lactose intolerant. I mix Hennessy and Hypnotiq knowing that the outcome is far from incredible. And I still buy XXL t-shirts knowing I ain't seen no parts of the gym, and I'm gonna resemble Pooh Bear after I eat my first meal. That being said, I sounded pretty convinced that the hoodrat loving life wasn't for me, right? Well, I'm hard headed! But after this encounter, I certainly learned my lesson.

In 2009, I did an internship in Orlando. For those of you who haven't been to Orlando, they have a special breed of hoodrat. They're gazelles for the most part. Hood gazelles are what I call hoodrats that are too beautiful and graceful to be labeled a rat. Not saying that rat is a fitting label for the rest of the population. If I could go through each hood and designate a spirit animal for each type, I would.

Well, my oldest brother told me I had to go to his house and get my niece and nephew cause the baby sitter had to go somewhere. I got there, and laawwwdddddd if the babysitter wasn't the baddest red hood hippo (big n graceful) that I've ever seen in my life. We're gonna call her Jennifer Thugson.

The next week I came over to my bros house again,

thirsting. cause I knew Jennifer would be there. So once my sister-in-law came home, Jennifer asked me if I could take her to the grocery store. *Damn right I can.* She got the groceries, and she asked if I wanted to come in. We was flirting a little bit n watching that Boosie movie (that's how I knew I had a winner on my hands). Then I went to the kitchen to get something to drink.

"Teddy, bring me something."
"What do you want?"
"Huh?"
"What you want?!"
"I can't hear you, huh?!"
"WHAT YOU WANT?!"

"UNH UNH HOL UP!! Nigga who the HEEEELLLLLLLL you yelling at?"

For those of you who don't know me in real life, just know I have a very low speaking voice. And no one hears me the first time, but they don't really get mad when I yell either because it eventually clicks that I've been responding for like, five minutes.

"You couldn't hear me. So I got louder so you could." "Yeen gon disrespect me like that!"

Me, in my calmest tone, "Umm… I wasn't. The hell wrong with you?" "NO YOU NOT CUSSIN' AT MY ASS TOO!" She stormed off to her room. At this point, I thought I just hurt her feelings. So I went after her to her room to apologize. I got about, a fourth of the way down the hall and I hear, "That's alright, cause I got something for ya ass."

"Wait…what?"

Her ass comes BARRELING out her room with a hammer like Thor-a Winslow.

"That's the LAST muthaf*ckin time you gon raise yo voice at me!" "Oh shit."

Then I run for life. I wasn't thinking fast enough, so I ran in the bathroom and locked it. I didn't know how I was gonna get outta this one

"NIGGA, YOU CAN'T STAY YA ASS IN THERE ALL DAY!" "Put that damn hammer down, I'll come out." "NIGGA, NEVER!!"

But, when a door closes, a window opens. Literally cause there was a window in the bathroom.

I'm short doe. And the window was kinda up there. But I stood on the toilet anyway and knocked the screens out the windows. I proceeded climb through, motivating myself.

C'mon Teddy! You got this! Almost there! I got to my shoulders and realized nothing else was gonna fit through that window. *Teddy… with yo big ass.*

"NIGGA! Did I hear you just try to climb yo BIG ASS thru that lil ass window?!" Hoodrat cackle.

Me, frustrated, "HO SHUT UP! THIS DON'T CONCERN YOU!!"

"HO?!?!"

DAMMIT, TEDDY! I smacked myself in the head 'cause I knew I just messed up.

Next thing I knew; the damn hammer came through the door. And honestly, I almost shit myself. THAT was probably the realest shit has ever been in my life, when she ruined her OWN door to get to me. She really wanted to beat my ass with that hammer. I NEEDED to get the hell outta there. If she swung at that door one more time, she was gonna make it in here.

Had to think fast. So I ran up to the door and threw that bitch open. I let out a battle cry, similar to the Zulu warriors, and smushed Jennifer in between the door and the wall. The funny thing was, her hand holding the hammer was hanging out, but she couldn't swing it to hit me, so it was just dangling. The funnier thing was, I could see her face through the big ass hole she put in the door. And I used a combination of strength, adrenaline, and a fear turd I'd been prairie doggin' since she put the hole in the door to keep her wedged ~~with this door~~ while I figured out how to get the hell outta there. And I was looking at her through the hole in the door, her face turned to the side cause of how the door was on her. It was hilarious, but I had to get out that house. Then I was like, Damn *you so fine! Why you gotta be nuttier than squirrel shit??*

I kissed her on the cheek through the hole in the door and TOOK OFF straight to the car.

A week or so later, my sis-n-law called me. "I thought you liked Jennifer? How come you don't come round no more? She said y'all had a minor disagreement but she's still interested."

Her risking it all with a hammer is considered a minor disagreement? So yea. I learned two things that day. One, hoodrat Infatuation is dangerous, especially for those not equipped for that life. Two, you have to learn how to live amongst hoodrats, cause they ain't going anywhere. So whatever you do, don't cuss at one or call her a ho.

My name is Teddy Belafonte, and I am an ex hoodrat addict and a hoodrat survivor.

Teddy & Bobby Go To Popeye's

When I was working in Orlando, I often found myself with time on my hands and nothing constructive to do. One day, me and my homie and co-worker Bobby Drake, one of the coolest brothers in Tuscaloosa Alabama, were both off work. We had nothing to do, had not a single f*ck to give, and just got paid. We had to do something. So we did something amazing. We played super smash brothers. Then we got hungry. Didn't want McDonalds, didn't want Subway. We thought about KFC, and that sparked a brilliant idea.

"BRUH!! We gotta find a Popeye's."

So, we got on the iPhone and looked for the nearest Popeye's. It was about thirty-five minutes away, but we were down for a mission. His map on the GPS got dark, which told us we were going to the hood. (Bet y'all ain't know iPhones had that feature?)

So we headed out the apartment complex, and we got 86 feet down the street when these two white girls walked in the middle of the street. One put her hand out like Prince Akeem. DAFUQ?!

I rolled down my window, ready to cuss they ass out something mean. "Sorry, we're french CP's (interns). Can we get ze ride to ze Walmart??"

You almost got yo ass flattened for a ride to Walmart?! I like y'all.

So, they got in the back and made it 20 feet before they said, "Thank you guys so much. We give you guys sex?" Well, that escalated quickly. And I wasn't mad at it. Us, "Oh WORD?!"

I would LOVE to tell you we took down two French girls in a PT Cruiser and dropped em off at Walmart. I would ABSOLUTELY love to. But we just dropped them off at Walmart because French women apparently own the troll title.

So, NOW we're on our way to the streets of Orlando. Yes, Orlando has a hood. And it gets real.

The funny thing is that there's no gray area on your way to the hood. You literally go from Universal Studios, to a Trick Daddy video in 3.5 seconds. It's amazing.

We finally got to Popeye's and behind the register I saw Missy Smelliot. 5'10 and 240 lbs of straight Floridian hoodrat. I told you Florida has a different breed of hoodrat. It's really nothing you've ever seen in Virginia or North Carolina or where have you. The hoodrats there are ride or die. Actually, why do I need to explain this to you? You've seen Khia. You know exactly what I'm talking bout. Missy had these thick ass, surprisingly pretty dreads, mouth slugged out, and tattoos saying RIP to everyone but Redd

Foxx. She eyeballed me all the way to the register. A part of me was hoping that Bobby was the one she was eyeing so lustfully. Hell ALL of me hoped that.

So, when I get to the register she goes, "What can I getcha baby?! Witcha chunky cute self." O__O

Thank you???

I placed my order, which was MASSIVE cause I had no idea when I'd be back. Bobby did the same and we waited for our order. Once we got our food, we sat down to go cunningHAM, but we forgot the main ingredient. Hot sauce.

Bobby went up to the counter and asked for it. And I hea6r THE WORST thing I've heard since "Did you hear Flex Alexander is playing Michael Jackson in his new movie?"

"Yea, you can have some, but ya friend gotta come over here and get it." No shame, at all.
"Ha, ha."
"Ha, ha, hell."

So, he came back over and laid the bad news on me. "Welp! Guess we ain't eatin chicken with hot sauce."

Then I realized what I just said was blasphemous. So I went over there. "Here go ya hot sauce, baby." She put her hand out, and every time I reached, she moved it further. So I leaned over the counter for it.

And...
And...
And...

This broad kissed me in the mouth. My WHOLE mouth. I was distraught. I was offended. I was...slightly turned on. Minus the fact that it tasted like pennies, Newports, and years of promiscuity,

Missy had game.

So, after the hoodrat employees of Popeye's stopped laughing, I got my hot sauce and used it and the chicken to ease the confusion. And JUST when I thought this night wouldn't get any weirder than it already had, this super feminine dude walks in wearing Coogi and sequin. It was a combination I had never seen in my life. He was tall and lanky, had long permed hair and a beard. He looked like a combination of "Hey Ya" Andre 3000 and the man upstairs. So, it's only right to refer to him as "Sweet Teasus." He walked in with two nice looking hood bunnies. Not quite hood gazelles, but they could get it. Of course me and Bobby glanced over at 'em, and they looked back.

So Sweet Teasus started walking towards us, and we thought he tryna buck. So we kept calm.

"I see y'all looking. Y'all boys like what y'all see?? They certainly like what they see."

Us, "……"

"Y'all boys ain't gotta be shy now, they play nice. And they'll take good care of you." I asked, "YOU A PIMP?!" Hood bunnies let out hoodrat nose laughter. "Don't be advertising my shit boy. Y'all interested??" Bobby, "NOPE! We bout to be out!"

Me, "Well, let's hear em out. I mean, you ARE a marketing major. Maybe you can give em some tips." Bobby wasn't with the shits. So, we finished up, hopped in the car and LEFT.

…I wonder if Missy ever thinks about me.

How You Gon Pimp A Pimp?!

I had the pleasure of being the Greatest Man at my cousin/brother Stevie Blunta's wedding. Twas beautiful. But I wouldn't be a good Greatest Man if I didn't send Stevie out with a bang. We were in DC; so where else would you take a man on his last day of freedom?? Damn right we went to Shtadium!

For those who don't know Shtadium, it is a very popular strip club in DC. And I'd never been, so I had to go and get my budgeted trick on.

Stevie is a religious man. We all are. But he's a religious one-woman man. Which is great, but he initially didn't wanna go to the club. I was HURT.

His fiancee kept telling him to go. She wanted him to go. He wouldn't go. So after the wedding rehearsal I devised a plan. "Steven Q. Murkel, Cooley, Goliath, and Shimmy SupaFly Snuka, we're gonna kidnap his ass." Cooley is my homie, my ride or die. I love him to death. But he can be a bit airheaded at times, bless his heart. I grabbed Stevie, threw him in my backseat, and leaned against the door. I called Cooley and gave him a simple order...

"Aye! I got him! Go to the other side and block the door." "Block YOUR door?"
"Yea, so he can't get out."
"Oh… what?? Ight."

Stevie got out the other side of the car.
"Yo, I think he's gettin out." Epic facepalm.

So Goliath pulled his Caprice up, and we tried this
again. We wrapped his ass up and threw him in the
back and took off. We were broke, so we had to go
to the bank first. Murkel was HYYYPPPEEE cause
he'd never been to a strip club. He was 27, had two
degrees, but could be fairly awkward. That's my boy.

We got to stadium and Goliath paid $20 to get his car
valeted. I parked on the street. We waited outside,
and the bouncer looked at Murkel and told him, "I
can't let you in with those sweatpants."

A new hustle.

Cooley had on a t-shirt and shorts. So I asked if he
could get in. He said yea, but he gonna charge him
more. Cool. What's a couple extra dollars to a
childless Teddy Belafonte? So, we had to work on
Murkel. Goliath went to his car and miraculously
found a pair of slacks that were balled up in his gym
bag. Murkel put 'em on, and they big as hell on him,
so he was out here looking like T-Boz.

We get patted down and FINALLY we're in the got
damn Shtadium. Beautiful hoodgazelles everywhere,
moving gracefully down the pole.

The bouncer looked at Goliath and charged him $40

for not having a collared shirt. Dude looked at me and said, "You got boots on, $60. And $60 for ya boy too (Cooley). I could've charged him $80."

The Hustle Strikes Back.

I was HURT, mainly 'cause I told Cooley that I'd look out for him before we got there. So I dropped $120 before I could even tip these gazelles. I finally got in, and I was amazed. I saw no C-section scars, no child birth stomach, no bullet wounds. No struggle at all. Did see a lot of silicone though, but these big city strippers.

I was working in my head how I could tip accordingly and get my drink on 'cause I saw Snuka with a drink in his hand. I got to the bar and paid $11 for a Heineken. So I made that ONE bottle last the whole night, taking the smallest of sips. Snuka paid damn near $20 for a tequila sunrise.

Goliath came up to me and said, "You wanna go half on a table dance for Stevie? They're $20 a song."

"Yea, I can do that. Let's get him three songs."

So two skrippers came over, Jennifer and Mary J Fried. They said, "y'all gotta make it rain so we work harder for ya boy." So we was tipping and I was lookin at Jen. I said to myself, "She sure does have a skrong ass face." But it being dark, I ignored it. I kept tipping so my boy could enjoy himself. Murkel was with Mary J having the time of his LIFE. Her titties knocked his glasses of his nose, and he ain't even notice. He just had 'em hanging on to his ears, dangling round his mouth, looking like a kicker facemask. Goliath was dropping singles one by one. "Work...twerk...get it...this b*tch is a man."

So. now I can tell you Jennifer last name is Manhandiston. Money stopped. Like I said, it was dark, and the strobe lights were somehow avoiding her. Then the light hit just right, and her face was indeed a lil sir-ish. I was staring at her to make sure I ain't sign Stevie up for *the Crying Game* before he got married. Then she said, "Baby if you keep on staring, Imma make you lick it."

My jaw dropped.

"Guhl you MIGHT be a boy! I ain't puttin my mouth nowhere!" Now I was done. Then the bouncer told us if Stevie didn't get up, he's gonna charge him for another song. I tried to make his ass get up, and Manhandiston said, "He can't get up until the song is over."

I was gettin' pimped. Return of The Hustle.

Goliath tried to give the dude the $60, and he said that since the strippers touched all of us, we each gotta pay $20. The Phantom Hustle. Attack of the Hustle. Bruh, REVENGE of The Hustle. The Hustle Awakens. I got T.I. in a Yoda robe sitting on my shoulders screaming, "Dough you get, or die you will." I was getting hustled so hard. There were six of us. You do the math. After we paid, we each had $5 left. We planned to spend it wisely.

Murkel found him a redbone and POSTED RIGHT IN FRONT OF HER. He did not move. The man upstairs could've told him that he was collecting him for the Rapture, and he still would not have moved. We all decided that we had been pimped hard enough, so we were gonna leave. I went up to Murkel and tell him that we're about to leave.

Here's what killed me. You know what he said?

"Ight man, I'll catch up with y'all later," he said, never breaking eye contact from the stripper. "Y'all take it easy." This…nigga…had…no…driver's license. He had no money for a cab. This was before Uber was a thing. He lived nowhere near walking distance. That's what happened when you watched the Best Man too much. We had to drag his ass outta there. I honestly felt like crying. And outside of tears of juicy booty joy, I had NEVER cried at a strip club. Whole time, Stevie got this bullshit ass grin on his face, 'cause he really just wanted to go to Olive Garden. This dude got free lap dances AND the last word?! Blessings. The moral of this story is: look past the struggle, the scars, and wounds, and go visit your local run down strip club. They are way humbler, AND they appreciate your support, AND you can come as you are.

Strip Club Etiquette and Hacks

Since trying to get a grip on this adulting thing for the past couple years, I haven't had the funds to enjoy the strip club like I used to. But BTR (Before The Responsibilities), I was in the building enough that I became a bit of a connoisseur, and was able to always have a great time no matter the situation. Sadly, I've noticed that some people just go about the strip club ALL WRONG, and hopefully I can learn ya something. Disclaimer: This did NOT happen at Shtadium, but did at another magical gentleman's club.

1. *Don't Sit At The Stage If You Have No Intentions of Tipping.*

Seriously??? Why do you think there are seats at the stage, and then couches on the other side of the club? Generous patrons get to sit at the stage. Broke boys need to migrate to the back. I mean, be considerate. The stripper on stage is trying to make money, she sees you sit at the stage and thinks you are ready to share the wealth. She twerks on over to where you are, and starts bussin it for you out of the kindness of her heart and the hungriness of her pockets, and she awaits some gratification. Alas, you're a dickhead. Please don't play with emotions.

2. *STOP Mean Mugging.*

I'm assuming you're straight, I mean you are at the strip club. Look like a straight male in a room full of titties and cheeks. I'm not saying stand around cheesing like a damn Cheshire Cat on cocaine, but damn my dude, smirk, grin, smize bro, SOMETHING! Ain't no stripper gonna approach aggression. You have a burgundy ass aura around you. MAKE THAT SHIT GREEN BEFORE YOU GO TO THE CLUB!!!

3. I'ma throw you a lil tip that you may not be aware of: get 40 ones from the door. Put 20 in your pocket, keep the other in your hand, but hold so it looks like you got a good amount of money. Sit AWAY from the stage and REMEMBER to get your aura in check. A stripper will see you chillin, come over and see the money and give you a lil personal show. It'll only cost you $5 at the most. Do that until you're content. Then, sit at the stage, and do the same thing with the money. Slowly tip dollar by dollar. She has no clue when the money will stop, but she'll stay round you as long as she sees green paper in ya hands. You're welcome.

4. *NEVER Ever Ever EVAH*
Get Trashed at a Strip Club.

I've seen some terrible tragedies coming from people fooling with that devil water. One dude was with his "boys" and I'm pretty sure it was his first time in the club, cause he was hovering round this one stripper, eyes cocked like the University of South Carolina. He started dancing with her, rubbing on her thighs and had NOT ONE dollar in his possession. Ole girl looked at the Ruben Studdard sized bouncer, and he proceeded to fold his drunk ass up and toss him

outside. His "boys" stayed in the club til it closed…
in December. Watch who you roll with to the strip
club. Another time I seen this dude take shots of
kerosene i'm assuming. He sat down in his chair and
in the corner of my eye I see a red flash. That red
flash was the chair he was sitting in going airborne
after he rolled out of it. And then he laid there,
motionless. Every gyrating ass on stage came to a
halt and then followed a crescendo of "OH SHIT!"
Did the bouncers feel sympathy? NOPE. Dude got
propped up against a fire hydrant. Don't go to the
strip club alone either.

5. If a few dollars randomly fall off the stage and into
your vicinity, it is OK to re-rain. Recycling is good
for the hoodrat environment anyway. But under
NOOO CIRCUMSTANCES can yo triflin ass pick it
up off the floor and put it in your pocket. Have you
no shame?! YOU JUST STOLE A PAMPER!! And
don't think you'll get away with it. Strippers, DJ's
and bouncers all have eagle vision. You will get
called out and hemmed up for a dollar. There's more
to life.

6. *Don't Expect VIP Privileges*
On A Dollar Menu Budget.

Doesn't matter how attractive a stripper finds you,
how fresh you may be, she will not walk away from
scattered showers to show yo broke ass any special
attention. If y'all were at the club, aye, you'd
probably take her home. But fam, she at work. She
don't go to The Cookout when you managing and

steal hushpuppies and cheerwine from you. Don't have her lose money. Again, be considerate.

7. *Don't Try To Outdo The Strippers.*

Ladies y'all thought I wasn't gonna show y'all any love didn't you? Toooo many times I've seen them allow girls on the stage for fun, after they got some liquid courage in 'em, and they SWEAR they just came back from Rio representing the USA in twerk. But their rhythm is equal to that of Ellen Degeneres' audience. Leave it to the professionals. And yes, I watch Ellen.

8. *Keep Ya Mouf To Yaself.*

The fact that I even had to tell y'all that disturbs me to my soul. Do I really have to explain myself? I know ya mammies told you to not eat food off the floor. If she warned you bout that shit, don't you think that f*ckery of this magnitude can cause serious harm to yo life? You haven't an iota of a clue where the hell that girl been.

9. *Don't Hog the Strippers.*

Sharing is caring. If the brother next to you has intentions on tithing, LET HIM. Strippers rotate. She'll be back for your money shortly. Dudes will get a girl in one section of the stage and will NOT let them leave the vicinity. I mean damn can she at least change her outfit? All that damn sweat, thirst, and ass cheese accumulating in her G String ain't a bit sanitary. Once again, BE CONSIDERATE! Dance, dance, pass.

10. *Don't Fall In Love.*

I saved this for last cause this problem is real. Don't be ashamed, it's not just happening to you. Hell, T-Pain made a song about it. Plenty of people have gotten mesmerized by the sight of a hoodgazelle sliding gracefully down a pole. It happened in the *Best Man* too. Well, it worked out for him (Harold Perrineau wins a lot though. Seriously have you seen Claws?). BUT! For the most part, leave those feelings in the club. If you bump into the stripper while she out making groceries, let that stripper make groceries in peace. Don't feel that you can get her number and set up dates and shit. It does not work like that. She's using your money to buy golden nugget cereal, the toppest of Ramen, and bologna without the red ring (cause she's classy like that, and that is the ONLY connection y'all will ever have. Let's think ahead: "Daddy when did you first meet mommy? When did you know you were gonna marry her?" Lie to your children if you want too, I bet that stripper loving guilt will eat thru your liver.

My name is Teddy Belafonte, and thank you for letting me be your strip club guide.

Be Better Than Me

I'm not sure if I've told y'all before, but if it's one thing the kid doesn't handle well, it's stress. I like to make myself busy so I don't have to deal with it. One of the things I make myself busy with happens to be strippers. Of the hood rat persuasion. Would I suggest it? Nope. Be better than me.

Last year, I had shut it down with a female I'd been seeing and was kinda bummed about it. So where did I head? Oh yes. I went to the sunken city of Thotlantis to surround myself around the finest, most available hood gazelles in Virginia. Aka the strip club. On a Monday night. Be better than me.

I walked in. There's a chick on stage who either gave birth before she got on, or planned on doing so after her set. There's an old creepy white dude in the corner. There's hood gazelles grazing at the bar. And then there's me.

I walked in, paid, and the DJ gets my attention. He said, "I mean…. you're basically the only one here. Anything special you want me to play?"

"Just throw some Big Krit on and I'll be good."

Girls on stage danced and their set is over. I think the DJ wanted to let me know how sad it looked that I was in there solo, because even though he's five feet away from me, he chose to get on the mic like, "Um... anything else you wanna hear man?"

On the mic bruh? You gotta advertise my loneliness? Bruh hit me with a shoulder shrug of extreme elevation. I was salty. But I ain't even leave. "Just turn on some 2 Chainz and let it ride fam."

Be better than me.

I grabbed me a Pepsennessy (soda and that magical brown liquor) from the bar and partook in a Newport. A hood gazelle with a little case of dandruff sat next to me. I'll call her Anita Flaker.

"Hey baby, can I have a light?
"Of course."
"You OK? Out here on a Monday. When did she leave you?" She took a drag of her cig.
"Damn. Last week."
"Aww, you want a dance?"
"I just came here to sightsee. I'm not even in the mood for all that. But yea, I want one."

Be better than me.

Went in the back. Got twerked on to the honorable Yo Gotti. Came back out to sightsee some more and Ms. Flaker sat next to me again.

"Did you like the dance?"
"Yea it was dope, thanks."

"Do you have IG?"

"Yea."

"OMG, you should totally follow me. You know, you can hit me up sometime."

"Word."

 I'd like to say I didn't pull a Myron from Player's Club. I'd like to say it.

BE.
BETTER.
THAN.
ME.

Teddy & The Princess of R&P

From the age of 22 to 24, my dating game was so strong. I got me a Plenty of Fish and an OkCupid account and just had the glow. Around this time, I was getting a little popular on Facebook and had just started blogging, so girls who curved or flat out ignored me in high school and college would hit me with the "lmbo :)" on my statuses. I felt like I had the sauce. I decided to take advantage of the "lmbo :)."

One young lady flirted with me in college for a semester then STOPPED. But I'm a sucker. And I'm hard headed, so when I joined my church and saw her there, in my head I was dropping all kinds of early 90's cheers like,"awww sookie sookie now!" as she hugged me. Then she commented on one of my statuses with "Lmbo :)" "WHO DA MAN!!"

Theeennnn I get that, "hey stranger," message. BOOMSHAKALAKA! I invited her out for unlimited breadsticks and salad. And of course, she started digging the kid. At that time I was childless, and waiting tables full time, so my money ain't fold. Still lived with my mom's, but you can kiss my ass, so there's that. Anywho, at my job, two of my coworkers, Chadam Vinatieri and LeAnn Dimes, were getting married. I had the honor of being the only black dude invited to the wedding. I'd never been to a white wedding. So, OF COURSE I WAS GONNA GO!! I just needed a date. So I hit up showty. I got dressed in my finest linens. Fresh baldy, beard handcrafted by the heavens. I went to pick her up, and you would've thought it was prom night. Mom Dukes outside grinning and waving. Ole girl came out flawless. Curls Bankhead Bouncing. Summer dress on. I was hype. And then, I was a stereotype. See, I was the Greatest Man at my cousins wedding a few months before, and I remember sitting in the pastor's office for thirty minutes because it started late. You know it's her big day, she wants to look perfect, and she need to hear ten, "Yaaasss bitch"s, before she puts her veil on.

Not this wedding bruh. Not this one at all.

It was outside at a country club. We pulled up. They was giving vows, bruh. I could see it. No way in hell I was enforcing that stereotype and strolling in there. We just gon sit inside and get a head start on this here bar. Swapping one bad look for another. An usher was standing next to me inside the country club, cutting his eyes over at me.

"Sooo...you know the bride or the groom?"
"I actually know both. I work with them."
"Really?! YOU WORK AT MUSTY CRAB?!"

Yessah Massa, shole did.
Luhz me enough to let me tend to his frenz n'em and feed em some good ass crab cakes.

So let's not make taupe people uncomfortable today this is a joyous occasion. Back to the date.

I asked what she wants to drink.

"Weeelll I normally go for tequila, but I have this app that picks drinks for me." Patti LaBelle's spirit whispered softly in my ear, "If... Only YOU KNEW." First drink was a Cosmo. I got a Pepsennesy of course. Then I went to beer. Gotta play it safe, ya know. She got wine. I got another beer. She got a woo woo. I got another beer.

We got up to toast the lovely couple. She started feeling it. We took some blurry ass photos. I was ready to get on the dance floor and sweat this out.
They started to serve us salads. Good ass looking salads too. Full of all the necessary additives to make em bright and beautiful. But first my boss, Bony Soprano, decided he wanted to change the game up and see what folk was made of.

"AYE, PATRON SHOTS ON ME!!"

I couldn't take a Patron shot. She couldn't either. The devil was moving. Still took the shots. Went back to the crayola salad. Salad was good as hell. My big ass ain't EVER enjoyed a salad like that. Food was too good to be true. I need to go to taupe weddings more often! Then Showty said, "I have to pee, but I don't know if I can make it to the restroom."

47

"I can princess carry you, and pretend you hurt yaself. "Um, gimme a second." "Take ya time."

Then I looked at Showty's face.

o_O
"...what?"
O_O
"Bruh..."
"I did it."
"Please..."
'I...peed."

So now I can call her PeePee Winans.

"Stand up."

Pee was all over the seat. I was having a good time, and her dress was short so I figured, my nasty ass, she might be alright. I ran to the bathroom and came back. The light hit her seat just right that the puddle of pee beneath it was gleaming as if to say, "Bitch you thought." "Take me home please."

"I'm on it."

She apologized the whole way home. I actually wasn't mad. I liked Showty that much I was willing to look past the piss. PTP. I was still a sucker. I had bought a stuffed animal for her in 2012 BP (Before Piss). So I swung by my house, since it was on the way. And this is why it doesn't pay to be a sucka.

I was driving down the road. And I heard a sound like someone spitting sunflower seeds. Then I saw that beautiful ass salad on my dashboard. She tried to hide throwing up by making quiet noises. First stealth puke I've ever witnessed, bruh. I got to my house, tryna be in and out. The ONE TIME my family wanted to be on a sitcom and congregated in the living room I strolled in with alcohol sprinting out my pores. Mom Dukes told my sister to drive us home. Whatever. Let's get this show over with.

One more sucka move fore I go. I was in the backseat, chilling. But wanted to show her I was still willing to look PTP (past the piss).

I went into WaWa and bought her a Ginger Ale. I came back to the car, and she's pretty much drunk, cutting me off to my sister. "Like, I'm pretty. I'm in college. I'm graduating soon. This isn't what I'm supposed to be doing." I said, "True."

After a while I realized she had NOOOOOO idea I was in the backseat. "And I just, I don't think I'm ready for a relationship. I'm not. And I don't wanna do this to Teddy. But when you see Teddy, tell him I'm sorry." "Right here, PeePee."

She texted her mom a bunch of gibberish, so instead she called her. "PeePee, what's wrong?"
"Heeeeyyyyyy Moooommm."
"Are you drunk?"
"Heeeyyyy, I'm coming home now."

So Mom Dukes was in the military, and had no tolerance for bullshit. I walked her to the door. Explained the open bar. Apologized 100 times. She still wanted to whoop my ass. Only reason she didn't was because she probably couldn't figure out whose ass to whoop first. And I roooooollleeeddd up outta there before she made her decision.

I hit PP up the next day. Another sucka move. Making sure she was ok. She said she owed me dinner and a car detailing. Then she disappeared.

She stopped texting. Ignored me on Facebook. BRUH SHE STOPPED GOING TO THAT CHURCH!!! PeePee, if you're reading this, after AAAAWWWLLLL THAT, I still would have looked PTP. You was that dope. I was that big of a sucka. It's still all love though. Urine my heart.

The Dangers of Online Dating

So. There was this girl that sent me a friend request on Facebook. I thought she was cute, so of course I hit that accept button. She was plus sized, and I'm a supporter of the BBW, so I was all for it.

We had a lot of conversations on the book and I thought she was cool. One day she put the conversation on her back doe, and said that she wanted to go to the movies with me. So we set the date. I was in Raleigh with my pops at the time for fall break. So him and I went to our favorite spot to get elbow deep in some pork before I went to go pick her up. I promise you that sentence has something to do with this story, and I'm not just being fat.

Later that day, ole girl texted her address and then she immediately called and was like, "Hey just to clear some things up, you ARE paying for me right?"

Red Flag #1.

I put the address in my GPS, and it sent me to West Buttcrack, North Carolina. It was actually somewhere in Garner, but I've lived in that area for ten years and never seen this part, EVER. All I saw was trailers and red clay. Like, how fast was I going and in what direction, 'cause I swore I saw Zora Neale Hurston checking the mail. I was time traveling! I just said a prayer and rang the doorbell.

Which didn't work, duh. Hadn't been invented yet, just a prototype. They could've at least had a cowbell out there or something.

Finally, her mom answered the door and I put on my gentleman swag. "Hello, my name is Teddy. I'm here for Showty." Moms invited me in, and asked where she knew me from. Come to find out, me and Pops sat next to her and her husband, and she told me she admired the way I took care of my dad. Her country fried husband came out, and they both couldn't get over how polite I was. It was just basic politeness. Like, I ain't take my hat off and hold it against my chest when I spoke to a woman. But Mom Dukes straight up told me I was a keeper. Keeper of what? Y'all tryna play Quidditch or something?

So ole girl finished getting ready, and she came out her room every bit of 5'10 (I'm 5'6 on a tall day). But I was cool with it 'cause she was cool. UN-f*ckin-til, we got in the car, and THE FIRST thing she asks me is, "How tall are you Teddy? 4'11?!"

That wasn't fair.

"I mean…. You should've told me you were this short! I could've stepped on you by accident!" Well now she was just roasting me… "AND I GOT ON THESE HEELS?! I'M LIKE 6'3 NOW!"

Well they were kitten heels, so let's relax.

I've never had a problem with my height. But she was like, sitting shotgun, just roasting my ass. She made like, four more short jokes before we even left the trailer park. THEN! To make things worse, I was driving my PT Cruiser at the time, and she got wedged between the dashboard and the seat. I was tryna tell her that the seat handle was different than a usual seat handle, but while I'm explaining myself, she just forced the seat back. That works too, I guess.

So while I'm applying cocoa butter to these burn marks I got from all her jokes, I drove past this shopping center and then, "OOHHH SUBWAY CAN WE STOP THERE AND TAKE IT TO THE MOVIES PLEASE?!?!?!"

Girl, you lucky this movie only costs a dollar, or you woulda been chilling at the crib.

When we got to the theatre, she started begging me for Reeses Pieces and a blue slurpee. NO! While we were watching the movie, she turned to me and said, "Teddy don't you wanna put your arm around me?"

"Naw...naaaaaaw, bruh. I'm too short." I had to let the hurt out. On that looonnnggg ride home, she looked at me and said, "Maybe the movies weren't a good place to go to get to know someone." I mean... I certainly learned enough.

"Where are you from originally Teddy?"

"North Florida."
"Oh. Is that why you're so short?"

THAT WASN'T EVEN A GOOD ROAST!! Still salty tho. Drove her back to the past so fast I passed The Watsons going to Birmingham.

The [Over] Thinker

Picture a statue of me in that classic ass pose.
Dope right?? Anyways...

I always get good laughs out of this story. I
personally don't find it funny, but y'all can laugh at
my misfortune. I've always been one to overthink
EVERYTHING. Even little things like standing up
in class to go to the bathroom. "What if I trip over
that table leg?" or "What if the teacher calls me out
and embarrasses me?" Yea it's sad. I do it all the time
though. So there was this girl that I was pursuing
around 2012. I'd known her for a while, but never
made a move. She was really dope though, so I gave
it the old college try.

After a couple dates, she agreed to be my Valentine.

It wasn't OFFICIAL official, but I figured it'd be a
nice gesture to get a stuffed animal and some
chocolate. But some middle class chocolate cause I
didn't wanna send the wrong signals. A Hershey bar
means, "I wasn't really thinking bout you. This was
just at the counter when I went to get my black n
mild, but enjoy that shit." Figaro Rochelle or
whatever those expensive ass chocolates are called
that come in the 14 karat gold wrappers means "I
plan on putting a ring on your finger once you finish
chewing."

So I aimed for the middle and bought some chocolate turtles.

See how I was over thinking?

So I got that and this stuffed basset hound (cause I know she wanted a dog) that was holding a heart. But I had to dig through the shelves to find one that had a decent message on it because the other ones said, "I Love You" and, "Bear My Children." I think the one I bought said, "Hug Me." Or something along those lines.

So we went to eat and I was nervous the whole time cause I already had the whole evening thought out in my head of me saying the wrong thing and her storming out and going to get some goons. While I was playing this extreme scenario in my head, I wasn't paying attention that we were going to the same seat. So I knocked into her and I'm like, three times her size, so I thought she was gonna fall down and hit something like in Million Dollar Baby.

I REAAAAALLLLY overthink things.

So afterwards I was taking her home, and I planned on giving her the gifts cause they were in the backseat, and I was gonna grab them and try to be smooth, but I couldn't figure how to do it. *Should I have some theme music playing while I do it? Get an ambience going?* But then I thought she was gonna gimme a speech, and call me lame and throw my shit out the window. And that's what I was dealing with the entire car ride. So I was sitting with one hand on the wheel, and the other in the backseat holding onto the gift bag for fifteen minutes looking like Weirdo of the Year.

I FINALLY got the courage to give it to her and what the hell did I do?!?!

I THREW the bag in her damn lap.

She jumped out of fear.

At that point, I just wanted to eject myself out my OWN damn car.

I don't really remember what happened next because I've purposely blocked it from my mind. And for a while, I had difficulty talking to her cause all I saw was me throwing random shit at her. So we ain't really talked much after that.

I should probably see a specialist.

Caution: Not Intended To Be Bout Dat Life

My name is Teddy Belafonte, and I have the worst luck with women. I don't know if I've done something in my past life, or if it's meant for me to document all of these fails I've compiled over the years. It's funny because all through college, it's been hit or miss. Like I've stated before, I didn't start thriving until my Facebook started to jump a little bit. So I was ho'n online for a while. And because I moved a lot in the past and I was in groups with folk from all over, I was long distance e-ho'n.

So there was this girl, Robin Thickens. She lived about an hour away, so I'd drive up there and kick it with her over the weekends. Except it wasn't just her. It was her folks, her, and her three big brothers. There was Omar and Mike Pex, two swole ass goons built like wisdom teef cause all they did was bench. And Fonzo, who was a little (a lot) touched. He had his high school diploma and worked full time, but when conversing with him you noticed a brief (not so brief) delay. Seems like every time I came over, all three of em lined up just to give me shit. I understand being a big brother, so I just rolled with the punches.

It always went like this:

Mike would say, "What's hannen,' Big BAAYYYBEEHH?" He'd reach for dap, then try to yank me up. I ain't no bitch, and I was still lifting weights heavy, so I always did the same to him.

Then, in came his brother. Omar.

"OOOHHH YOU THINK YOU BIG SHIT HUH?!"
He'd try to jump me, and I'd fight back. "Okay lil
nigga, I see you. Respect. When that cell closes
though, it's just me and you." Mike and Omar were
institutionalized. Jail was they second home.

And then, here came Fonzo.

"Hey Big Belly Billy!"

I'd sigh. "What's going on, Fonz?"

"HUH?! WHATCHA SAY?! TALKING SHIT?!"
Another sigh. "No Fonzo. You got it, bruh."

"Good! Beat yo ass with my bat!"
"Naw, I don't want that Fonzo."

Every time I came in, this was the back and forth. So
this one time, I went through the ritual and enjoyed
time with showty. Omar and Mike's boy Shanks
comes over the house for a session. He did time with
them before, and you could probably put together the
pieces of the puzzle as to why they called him
Shanks. So I was chilling, and Shanks came in with
a big ass thermal, big jeans, and raggedy air force
ones. In the springtime. He went in the back with
Omar, Mike, and Fonzo to spark up, and comes back
out an hour later. Another hour AFTER, Mike went
back to a gruesome discovery.

I heard Mike say, "HELL NAH BRUH!!! O, come look at this shit man."
Then Omar. "WHAT?"
"LOOK."
"BRUH."
"I'M SAYING."
"ON DA SET?"
"NIGGA, YES!"
"WHOO??!?!"
Then in unison "TEDDY!"

"Huh?!"
Mike, "BRING YO ASS!"

I went in there so confused. And so shook cause with all this anger, they grew another foot taller and added another thirty pounds of angry muscle.

Mike said, "WE had a whole pound of Bubba in the room. We left. Unbeknownst (learned this in prison) to us, someone came and took our shit. I'm thinking it was you. Now my feelings is hurt. cause see, we let you in our home out of the kindness of our hearts cause our sister likes you. So I'm hurt because you chose to steal from US. If you needed some change we coulda took ya on a run, but to just take from us and bite the hands that feed you... you just broke a few codes that woulda got ya DEALT WITH! On the inside. So, Ima give you a chance to fess up and tell me what you did with my pound."

"Bruh, I been on this couch the whole time. I didn't take anything." Then Omar said, " Ight, so something bout me and my brother, we don't like being lied to, bruh." "I'm not lying though."

Robin chimed in. "Why can't y'all leave him alone? He doesn't even smoke. He was with me the whole time. Did y'all ask Shank what happened????"

Mike responded. "I did two years with Shank. He wouldn't take from me." It was then I realized that being locked up together is a bonding experience for some folk. Sad truth. But these dudes was locked up for a reason. "I been right here. I have no place to hide a whole pound, bruh."

"Ok now I'm getting mad, bruh cause you playing now, bruh." When folk use bruh more than once, they are no longer in a good mood. Mom dukes decides to intervene. "Teddy, dinner ready, you want something to eat?" Mike, "Hell naw mama, don't feed that thieving ass muhf*cka."

"BOY SHUT UP."

I went in and got me a delightful plate of elbow noodles and neckbones. Then moms put her two cents in. "Baby, if you took it, now don't be afraid to admit it. It's not too late to repent now."

Et tu mama?!!

I swore to her I ain't take it.

I went back to the couch to eat. Mike said, "You ready to confess?" "Man I swear I aint take it. I ain't left this couch let alone this house. Ya boy Shanks was in and out the whole time he was here."

"Ok Ima have to bring out the big guns now. FONZ!!!" Fonzo, "Huh??" "Bat Signal!!" "YYAAAAAYYYYYY FINALLY!!"

Fonzo came down the hallway with this wooden bat that he was obsessed with and ALWAYS threatened me with, but I'd never seen it. I thought he was making it up. I was actually surprised they let him have one. And then I'm wondering, *does he have any bodies on that bat? Should I be fearful for my life?*

"Don't make me do it, Big Belly Billy."

So now I was sitting in front of these two huge brothers and Sloe Clark and the Batman. Now I was nervous cause ain't no telling how many empty threats he's made, or how eager he was to crack someone upside the head.

"Bruh!!! I ain't do it man. Please ask Shanks. PLEASE!" Then came in Omar, "See you bullshitting. Ima call this man so he can call yo lying ass out too." He called Shanks. "Shanks, Robin punk ass boyfriend came in here and stole our pound of Bubba and he tryna pin it on you. Get his ass."

"Oh...man. Naw, like, you remember I bet y'all fifteen honey buns on the game when we was locked up? Y'all only gave me five, so I figured the pound would make up for it. Y'all can get it back, I just need $100." How much is a damn honey bun worth on the inside?! Then Mike and Omar, again in unison, "DAFUQ?!?! Yea we gone come get it you at ya girl house?!?! We on the way."

Mike turned to me. "Ight, come on Teddy."

"Wait, where we going?"
"Nigga, we going to get our pound and to get revenge on Shank ass for us AND you. My bad, by the way."
"Yo bad by the way?!? Yall was finna kill me for something I swore to y'all I ain't do and that's all you can say?! "IS YOU COMING OR NOT?!?! cause if not, Ima think you had something to do with it."

Robin chimed in again. "Teddy, Just go with em."

Et tuski Booski?!

So they scared me into going round the way to Shank house. He come out, hands over the pound and apologized. Mike and Omar just started swinging on him. He was on the ground and Omar say, "Come on Teddy, get yo one!" "Wait, what?!"

Then Mike said, "This dude almost got you killed you better get some revenge."

63

DISCLAIMER: I, Teddy Belafonte have never been about this life. I ever so gently nudged this man with my foot a few times, and whispered, "Run, please. Just run." I'm a lover.

Last time I seen Robin or went up there, my face swelled up and my throat closed as soon as I walked into the house. I guess I'm allergic to betrayal.

Cue Jamaican air horns.
OOOOOOOOOOOOOOOOOOOOOOHHHHHHHHH
HHHHHHHHHHHHHHHHHHHH.

But for real Robin.
We could've had something special.

I Was Just Supposed To Pray & Sit Down

I was in the boonies with this girl I was talking to a while back, and one weekend, we decided that we were going to her church. This was a holiness church, COOLJC (Church Of Our Lord Jesus Christ). Very hands on, wanna be seen and heard. I love me some Jesus. But I'm Baptist, which is more chill than a holiness church.

So me and ole girl was at this church in the sticks, and this wasn't my first time there, so I wasn't uncomfortable. This particular service was different. The bishopwas preaching and pacing back and forth in his incredibly aggressive angry uncle-that-just-got-out voice. But I noticed I felt like I did the time I sat in front of mama as she opened a letter from my second grade teacher that contained a worksheet that I had written the F-bomb on because I was curious as to how it looked and forgot to erase it before I turned it in. That really happened, by the way.

So this Bishop was walking around, talking about how I should be ashamed that I drink, smoke, go out, dance with women, do the do, and listen to 8ball & MJG. He was talking to the entire church but the whole time I felt like he was staring directly at me. And every time he made a point, he scared me into praising the Lord. "Females don't know how to be ladies. Skirts so short, ya bend ova and catch a cold. TELL THE LAWD HALLELUJAH!"

O__O. "Holla, holla-looyah."

An hour passed and I still felt like he's looking at me, like JUST me. I was shook. I wanna vomit and go home and lay in bed until Tuesday. I contemplated a Terrence Howard tear so he'd stop looking at me.

Then he quieted down and I felt like I could breathe. I thought the service was almost over. ADD kicked in, and I was putting myself in random episodes of my favorite TV shows. Next thing I heard is, "Something, something, something. Come to the altar." Ole girl and her friend stood up, and so I do too. Me, being a Baptist, I thought it's an altar prayer when everyone goes up and they pray over everyone at the same time, say amen, and go back to their seat. I love those, cause what better way to start your week off? I was standing up there with like, fifteen other people. The Bishop then dropped this hammer on me, "That's admirable that you young folk can come up here and admit that y'all are sinners!"

Wait, what?

"So here's what I want y'all to do."

No.

"I want y'all to kneel at the altar."

Please stop.

"And don't get up until you speakin' in tongues."

NOOOOOOOOOOOOOOO.

I've never been one to be slain in the spirit. Don't get me wrong. The spirit moves in me, but I've never been one to shout, jump, and def never spoken in tongues. I was standing up, tryna figure out how I'ma get outta this. *Do I sit down now and risk the possibility of this church recognizing me as the devil? Do I fake it? I'ma just get down there and see what happens. It's never happened but maybe it's my time.*

As soon as he said that, this lady started going, "HALALALALALALALALALALALALALALALA LALA," and goes down on her knees.

Now, I've never been one to judge, especially in the church. But I said to myself, *Them ain't tongues.*

Was she in the spirit? Probably. Was them tongues??? No. She sounded like dude on the Chappelle Show, "LEMME HOLLA, LEMME HOLLA, HOLLA, HOLLA, HOLLA."

I got down there, put my head down, and prayed to myself. While the Bishop was up there going Smithfield Ham on everybody.

"TELL HIM YOUR SORRY! LORD, I'M SORRY FOR FORNICATING." O__o

"LORD I'M SORRY FOR DRINKIN' AND SMOKIN, WEED. LORD I'M SORRY FOR HAVING SEX WITH OTHER MEN!"

HU-WHAAATT?!

So I tuned him out and took that time to talk one on one and thank Him for everything, and to help me better myself, so forth and so on. Everybody around me was yelling and crying, and I sat there quiet. *Am I being judged??* I um, I didn't know. I knew I was too afraid to lift my head up, so I stayed down there.

Round this time, my knees were crying louder than that lady that was speaking tonsils. A man my size ain't posed to be kneeling like that longer than 45 seconds. You know I'm awkward right? I catched this MEEEAAAANNNN Charley Horse in my thigh.

"GEE ZUS!"

Shouldn't have said that, Teddy.

I saw one of the elders' shadow running over towards me. Why? cause he thought I was finally finna speak in tongues. He brought the holy oil out. I was not gonna fake it, so I just go back to my one on one time, thinking he was just gonna put the oil on my forehead and move on.

He put the oil on, grabbed the back of my head, and applied some Tongan Death Grip.

"C'MON, C'MON. LET IT OUT. C'MON NAH, LET IT OUT!" I just repeatedly said, "Thank you." He was interrupting my one on one.

He let me go. I thought I was in the clear. Nope.

He squat behind me, grabbed me. Like his hand was on my mitties right now. He said, "LET IT OUT," and I felt breath on the back of my neck. I jumped up so quick.

Bruh I ain't finna go to second base with you, outchea. Cut that out expeditiously.

He thought his job was done. I thought I needed a bleach shower. I went to my seat, and EVERYONE but the pastor and nurses are slain.

I really didn't know what to do, so I walked around the church continuing my one on one. This went on for another hour and half. My calves probably looked like they did a bid.

I was just posed to pray and sit down.

I Just Wanted Some Bojangles Doe...

Sooooo round my junior year of undergrad, I was chillin with your fav Baltimore goon in Steve Maddens, John TrAssaultYa, and my other friend, Flexence Atkins, a goonnette from The Bronx that somehow made it to Petersburg, Virginia. She's affectionately referred to as my estranged wife cause to the untrained eye, you'd think we were going thru a divorce that could only be seen in something written by Tyler Perry. That's just how we argue.

So we were studying, or supposed to be anyways, and we (me) got a taste for Bojangles. With the only one being in Hopewell, Virginia. Flexence begged to differ. And no matter how much I raised my voice, we still wound up in the McDonalds parking lot. And I was driving. My struggle.

So she went in McDonalds. While she's in there, me and John stood outside partaking in a Black & Mild. Some Matrix shades wearing dude (Whorpheus) walks up and asked to borrow a phone. I don't like folk touching my stuff, so I told that my phone is dead. Lie. John, being the good Samaritan he is, he let dude use his phone. And John walked away, to go to my car n get something. And this happened:

"Yo, I messed up, Mayne. Real bad mayne!" A single tear rolls down Whorpheus's cheek.

o_O

"Mayne, I pulled, he hit the flo, I seen blood and I RAN......... ight yo, peace." He handed me phone and walked away casually.

Me: O__O . For like... five minutes.

Then John came up. "What's wrong?"

"Umm... I've only watched the *First 48* a few times. But um... I'm pretty sure that dude just confessed to a murder on your phone."

The hilarious thing about John is that even when he's stressed or upset, or any emotion really, his facial expression reads, Zero f*cks given.

"Oh. OH... OOOHH ight. Yea, ight. Well shit...that's real. Uhhh...

He threw the phone on the ground. A-town stomped it. Then threw the phone down the gutter. To this day, I hope Whorpheus was going around playing a bad joke on people. But if he really did catch a body, we were not accomplices!

Bojangles was closed now, so I settled for something from WaWa. John's a vegegoonian (goon vegetarian, keep up), so he wasn't down for Bojangles anyway, he just wanted to ride. We went in, cop work, got out. On the way to the car, there's this big ass Tahoe a space over from my car and it's full of clothes n shit. This tiny black lady with this squeaky voice leaned out her passenger window aaaannnndddd this happens:

"Excuse me? Excuse me?

"Yes ma'am?" cause I'm a gentleman n shit.

"Are you stalking me??"

"...Beg your pardon?"

"Are you stalking me?!"

My slow ass. I was sitting there like, *"did I accidentally poke this lady on Facebook and scare her or something?"* And I started to feel bad.

Flexence responded, "Ma'am, no one is stalking you." "Oh I'll be damned! Somebody is stalking me! And YOU look like the person who's stalking me. His name is *Voldemort* from Norfolk State and he's a *Fraternity that I won't name* and I'm ready to fight back! I already got the sheriff and went to Fort Lee and now the military is looking into it. I'm getting ready to fax the president if it gets out of hand after that."

It finally clicked in my head.

Me: OooooOOOOOOOO... She's CRAAAZZYYY. I get it. There's nothing I can do to please her.

John said, "Miss. Relax. No one is."

Then Flexence, "John, just get in the car.

We left. I don't know if she ever got help. I don't know if Obama ever faxed her back. I don't know if she cleaned out that junky ass Tahoe. I don't know if Whorpheus ever got caught. I didn't know the details to Google the story.

What I DO KNOW is that none of this would've happened if we went to Bojangles.

Every Night At 11:11pm I Wish A MF Would

During my last semester of undergrad, I was so wrapped up in finishing my last few major classes, I had no social life. So my best friends on campus were in my major cause those were the same people I saw and struggled with every day. Even if we weren't in the same major we'd still be close cause we had some epic ass adventures.

This one adventure was probably the realest shit I've ever experienced.

Lemme introduce my fellow culinary goons though:

Billy Pistol. 6'3, 370 something pounds. Just big and seemingly menacing, but nicest guy you'll ever meet. My fellow country bruh from Caroline County, Virginia. If I got in trouble in class, it was probably because me and him were clowning on someone.

John TrAssaultya. My homie from Baltimore, built like John Coffee, which should intimidate you, but his Steve Madden shoes wouldn't let him. Be honest. Would you be scared of a dude in Steve Maddens??

This one particular night, we were in the city of Petersburg after class and were in a bad "I wish a MF would" mood, because we were working on a group project together and the professor kept screwin' with us. So we decided to take a drive out to Richmond, go to the mall, and blow off some steam.

We stopped by John's crib to drink a couple brews before we left. I walked outside because I left something in Billy's truck. It's dark out, and we were in the hood. So I was climbing my short ass in the truck, and when I got out and turned around, I was face to face with this crackhead couple. They were probably a combined weight of 94 pounds and a total of eight teeth all together.

Homie had on a Houston Oilers windbreaker and was using a necktie as a belt. Let's call him Kirk Stanklin. His girl, Grease Witherspoon, had on a St. Paul's hoodie and some of those stretch pants that just said "OOT" on the back of them.

Kirk said, "Look here big man, I don't want any problems and I don't wanna handle you, just gimme your wallet." Then Grease chimed in, "You tell him, baby." "Shut up, bitch. I'm working."

Me, "Huh??"

I was staring him down to see what he was holding under his jacket. I couldn't tell, but I knew it wasn't a gun. Crackheads can't afford 'em. "Gimme your wallet nigga and I won't hurt you. Don't play dumb, big man." "Show 'em what you got boo. He hardheaded."

You won't believe what he had.

But I'll give you a chance to guess. What'd you guess?? You were probably wrong. That man had the nerve to try to rob me with a frozen bottle of water. The distilled bottles you get from the grocery store. I immediately chuckled from the gut.

"Keep laughin' I'ma grudgeon ya big ass with this hard sumbitch." "Grudgeon?? (bludgeon)"

Meanwhile, John seen the lovely couple standing in front of me and he sneaked over to where I was. And I was studying my exit strategy. I figured since he weigh about 49 pounds, as soon as he cocked that bottle back, it's gonna throw him off balance. Then I would swing on his ass, and then front kick the shit outta his girl cause I can't punch a female. (I typically wouldn't kick one either, but she deserved it for supporting her dumbass husband.)

So now, John was unnoticeably standing behind them. He yanked the bottle out Kirk's hand and scurred the shit outta Grease cause her crackhead speed kicked in and she TOOK OFF!

Kirk Turned around. "OH GEESHUSH!!"

I grabbed him and hemmed his ass up against the truck. Billy FINALLY came out, and he ain't ask what happened. Showed no concern for me at all. First thing he said was, "NIGGA IF YOU DON'T GET THAT SCRAWNY BITCH OFF MY TRUCK!"

I didn't know you cared, Billy.

So I got his ass pinned against the truck, and we tryna figure out what to do. So Billy grabbed his gun that he ALWAYS had on him cause he wants street cred. That gun was emptier than Kirks mouth though; he sold his bullets for school books. Ambitious goon problems. So after we had a meeting of the minds, we decided to take him with us to Richmond. Threw his ass in the back. Had John sit back there with him to make sure he ain't jump stupid. When he got in, this fool actually asked for his bottle back. I kept pouring it out the window as it thawed, just to piss him off and waste his hard work. cause it had to be difficult for a homeless crackhead to freeze something.

"Where y'all cobbler eatin' jokers taking me?!"

"Shutcho ass up and ride. You shoulda left me alone." "Look, big man. I'm sorry bout that stuff in the past. Let's get our asses a clean slate."

The past?! Nigga, it was just ten minutes ago!

"Man I ain't mean to. Holidays coming up, I'm just tryna look out for my kids. (It was definitely damn near February.)" Then we just riding. It was quiet.

Until Kirk said,
"You boys been keeping up with da football?"

"Oh MY Gawd SHUT UP! Before I hit you with your own bottle." "I swear, I'm sorry big man. I ain't gon try to rob you no mo." "Bruh, we really should've just left your ass in The Burg. You so annoying!"

We finally made it to Richmond, which is about 40 miles from where we got Kirk. Put him out the car at Church's Chicken, but I formed a bond with him that night, so I gave him some words of encouragement.

"If you ever make it back to the Burg and I see you with another frozen bottle of water, I'm running ya ass over." Then pulled off.

True story. Well… Probably.

I don't know the statute of limitations for kidnapping. I can't afford legal troubles.

The L's We Hold Dear

My homeboy Timbagland is my best friend.

It started in 10th grade band class. We were both new to the high school, so we talked to each other just because we didn't know too many people. What I later learned is that what really makes a best friend is all of the bs you go through and manage to make it out together still thriving.

It was junior year, the two girls we were chasing (who happened to also be best friends) got mad at us for Lord knows what and just started dragging us on MySpace with subliminal bulletins. You know that stuff was traumatizing for high school kids especially when you see people responding with "Girl, he wack anyway, and everybody know who they talking about. What made it worse was that this happened right after my birthday on October 24th and right before his birthday November 1st.

During senior year, between my birthday and his, we were in government class taking a test. The thing that made me and Timbaglands so close is that we had the same sense of humor and loved messing with folk. His timing was a little off, though. So we're taking this test, and the teacher didn't know us from the year before, so she sat us next to each other. So, I was in the middle of a test that I actually studied for, and Timbaglands started smiling and leaned over to me and said, "Yo, Branden said that Jessica." The teacher ran over there and snatched both of our tests up and gave us zeros. I could've at least gotten a C on that bih. "Bruh, what did you need to tell me that was so important?!"

"Oh I was just gonna tell you that Branden said that Jessica looked like Scooby Doo."

Brrruuuuuhhhhhh

We noticed a trend from then on. Every year, between my birthday and his, we took some crazy L that we just needed to come together and try to help each other cope with. NegroBromance.

This one L we took though, I figured if we bounced back from it, there's a reason why I made this dude my son's godfather. So our boy Johann Sebastian Flockah had a show out at this bar in Harrisonburg, so we went out there to support. We out there enjoying the tunes. I saw this girl we went to high school with that I had a crush on. Pretty natural girl. Let's call here Hairy Washington.

Me and Hairy were catching up. I asked her if she came here with her man and she said, "Nooo, I'm single. Just out with some friends." So I was scoping, hoping my man Timberglands come through with an assist. "Where they at?" "They right there." So I looked over, and pretty much see Boyz II Men twerking off in the corner. So that's a no go on putting

Tim on. Hairy and I continued to catch up, and I offered to buy her a drink after she pulled her card out. I tried to be smooth and gently glide her hand back into her purse, but I was on that Hen dog and I knocked her card out of her hand. I bent over to pick it up the same time she did, and I head butted the hell out of her. "Lawd Geezus, I'm sorry!"

"No, it's ok. You didn't mean too."

One of her homeboys stormed over and claimed I hit her. "UNH UNH NUH UNH HOOOOLLLL UP!"

His drunk ass ran up on me, so I hit him with the flipper to keep him off me. Bad idea, cause the Rest of Boyzz II Men chimed in. "No THE F*CK YOU DIDN'T PUT YO HANDS ON MY BITCH."

"Yo Bitch????"

This dude came up to me with his boys. It was warm outside, so all of em had on tank tops and short shorts except the leader. Who had on a hoodie and was probably gonna do some Darth Maul ass reveal or something once he was ready to pop off.

So I was standing in front of the Slum Village People, and they all drunk and wanna whoop my ass. Their leader took off his hoodie, and bruh was like 6'3, 235 pounds, and all muscle. So I was face to face with Jevon Purse. "LIL BOY! I WILL MOLLYWHOP YO ASS RIGHT HERE!!"

The SVP, "YAAASSSS WE WIIILLLL HOOO."

Tim saw the confrontation and came over for support, but it's still four to two. Hairy was trying to intervene, but they drunk and they needed this fight. If they rinsed two big black dudes, it was definitely gonna give Slum Village People hella credibility. Tim whispers to me, "You think we got this??"

"Hell nah. Bruh, we gon lose this one. We are absolutely not built for this. Gay people got hands." "Ight. You take Jevon. I get the smaller ones, then we run out the door." "NIIIGGGUUUHHH! WHY I GOTTA FIGHT THE ACTION FIGURE?!"

So Tim and I were toe to toe with Slum Village People. Jevon was a whole foot taller than me. I couldn't reach bruh face. I had nothing. I was lost. At the most, I could release a fury of punches on his mid region, but I'd be hitting all six pack. It'd probably hurt me more. Tim was taller and solid, so he didn't feel the disadvantage I felt. He knew nothing of the struggle. In my head I was like…

Bruh what the f*ck you gon do?? He too tall to swing on. But you got the low ground. Then, lightbulb. *You know what you need to do.*

First thing that crossed my mind was a WWF classic, the Farrooq Spinebuster. I got my arms around Jevon Purse's legs, lifted him up, and EARTH that man with the strength of whatever embarrassment I would've felt by getting my ass whooped by somebody with both their thighs all the way out. Whatever I needed to do to NOT get jumped by Slum Village People. Tim just bulldozed the rest of Slum Village People til they hit the ground and ran behind me. We hit the door and ran to the parking lot. Made it to the car. Tim pulled off and hauled ass.

Then I said, "Bruh. EYE could've did that."
"Did what?! Save yo life?!"

"Save WHO life?! You was just clumsy and knocked a bunch of skinny niggas over. I saved you from Brock LYAAASSSnar." "I'm impressed, though. Excellent execution by the way. Your future kids will be thankful." We had a long drive home full of smoke, McDonalds, and laughter. Made vows that from that point forward, that would be the LEAST told story from the both of us.

The Dizzney Massacre.... Almost

While I was living in Orlando, I had five roommates. They were:

Prettyboy Floyd. The only other black guy in the apartment, which was rare. So I'm guessing they thought I was white. He was from New York and was a typical cocky, flashy New Yorker.

Small Blart. He was a tall, skinny, nerdy white boy from Oshkosh, Wisconsin. So you KNOW he's never been around black people. And you could tell. I think in his entire life, he's known about three black people, two of them being me and Prettyboy Floyd. He worked as a security guard on campus back at his school, so every day was an episode of cops.

Smellroy Jetson. My boy! Rich, country white boy from Baton Rouge. We chilled all the time doing dumb stuff. He didn't have an odor problem, just looked very similar to the beloved cartoon character.

Slacklemore. Sensitive artist type from Arizona. Always sketching when he was in a mood. Had hella girls chasing him while doing his internship, but he ignored all of them. I initially thought he was picky. He came out the closet a couple years later, but I'd like to consider myself as a progressive person of society. He's still my boy.

Last but DEF not least, The Creeperican.

Puerto Rican creeper, duh. Just, just listen.

Ahem. Creeperican was a socially awkward Puerto Rican guy from New York City. I felt bad for him when I first met him because he told me how he didn't have any friends in high school and always struggled to fit in. He didn't seem so bad to me. So I was like, "Hey my man, we can be boys. No problem."

Weeelllll, somewhere along our time as roommates, I think he got confused with some things. Initially, he would always offer to wash my dishes when I went to put 'em in the sink, or when I went to take the trash out he would always try to take it and do it for me. He was like that with all of us. We had a house meeting and just informed him, We WANT to be your friend. You ain't gotta be our butler to kick it, fam. So he just started kicking it. Cool, right? He missed his mark again. He became an asshole. A socially awkward asshole.

Friends mess with each other. It's a given. The length and strength of your friendship determines how hard you mess with your friend, right?

So I had a girl over in the living room, and we kicking it watching a movie. And in this movie, there was a scene where a guy um, showed himself some love and got caught. My company jokingly said, "You not touching me with the hand you do that with, are you?" I replied, also jokingly, "Nah I handle all that business with the left hand."

Creeperican, who just so happened to be in the kitchen during this exchange, decided that this is an opportunity to chime in. "Yea, he uses his RIGHT hand to play with his asshole"

Fam.
Bruh.
Sir.
Mon frère. Not cool. Not even a good joke. Whole mood changed. And so began the fall back era.

One day he came in the apartment, hella excited cause he just met this girl on the bus and got her phone number. I ain't really cool with him at this point, but I could tell he's excited, and I know what it's like when you need to get a win off of your chest, so I lend my ear.

"Dude, we were both going to get fitted for our uniforms, and she has the sexiest tattoo on her foot."

Obligatory, "Ok, I see you."

"Yea, I saw it while I was peeking through her fitting room door." Me, shook. "Oh shit."
"So on the bus ride back, I got her number, and guess what?" Me, still shook. "Yea?"

"She has five other roommates too! I'ma call her later and invite them over." He started calling her.

"Oh, it's later now?"

Folks. He called her four times back to back. Left a voicemail on the last one.

"Hey Dabby, this is James. We met on the bus. Just wanted to let you know, we're having a little get together at the apartment, and you and your roomies are more than welcome to join us."

She ain't even answer the phone and I could hear her losing interest. To my surprise, Dabby still came through with her roommates! We was all under 21, so we just sitting round playing Rockband and conversing. Out of six roommates she brought through, we hit it off with about four and a possible. Not bad. Two of her roommates were black, so I just jumped into conversation with whoever made eye contact with the kid first. We all exchanged numbers and said we would go hang out in a couple of days.

One night, Prettyboy, Blart, Slack, Smellroy, Dabby, a couple of her roomies, and myself went to this hookah bar in downtown Orlando. Creeperican said he hated the smell of smoke, so he decided not to go. Bad move on his part, cause assuming Dabby still had any interest in him, Smellroy swooped in and took all that at the bar. She was feeling my boy.

We went back to our apartment. Dabby bowed out cause she had an early shift. So we're back at the crib, turning up on like, four hard lemonades and sleep deprivation in the living room, scattered between the floor and the couch. Rambling, talking shit. Creeperican poked his head out the door and asked us to keep it down 'cause he has an early shift too.

We tried. We failed.

The rambling shittalking continued, and we got on the topic of how he went about trying to get at Dabby. Not even realizing how loud we were cause we're delusional at this point. He poked his head back out the door like, "Ya know. It's really hard to sleep with you guys talking shit about me. That's f*cked up." Slammed the door. Bruh was mad for real.

A few hours passed and we dosed in and out of consciousness. Finally, I woke up to his door opening up. I was playing sleep cause I was not too sure if he had something up his sleeve. I was laying on the couch with Dabby's roommate and I was whispering to her cause I was shook. I mean, we might had something coming.

I heard him going through the drawers in the kitchen, and I kept hearing the rattling of a pill bottle. My sleep drunk ass was thinking to myself like, *Yo, we got that big ass butcher knife in the drawers. He gonna kill us and then pop mad pills!! Just cause we talked about his sloppy shot formation.* So I sneaked my phone out while he went in the bathroom, and sent a mass text warning them about this massacre.

These drunk asses laughed at me. But I was sleep drunk enough to see this shit happening. I texted them an escape plan. They laughed harder.

I'm like, "Yo, if I wake up dead, I'ma be pissed off! I need witnesses, and y'all just steady laughing."

My black ass was surviving this horror flick. If y'all gotta go, y'all just gotta go. Soooooo....it turned out, Creeperican was making oatmeal and taking multi-vitamins. Oops.

I definitely became an enemy after that.

What NOT To Do During An Interview

I'm not too sure how other colleges got down. But while I was in school, whenever a company that was remotely related to my major came on campus, it was mandatory to schedule an interview. This may be hard to believe because I'm such an excellent storyteller, but interviews are my kryptonite. Complete, all-expense paid trip to Struggleville. I've gotten better in my age, but I'm still not where my grown ass should be. This one time, I had the performance of the night.

So this company, which shall remain nameless, was having interviews in the building that my major was in, and it was mandatory to sign up for one. So I woke up early, did some research on the company, shit, showered, shaved, did the "I AM SOMEBODY" speech in the mirror, and got there early enough to calm myself down cause I was nervous as all hell.

The lady called me in and asked me how I was, and I couldn't decide whether to say I'm fine, good, great, or well, so like an idiot I said, "I'm chillin." Then I put my head down and that's where it stayed for the rest of the interview.

I'm shy naturally, but freshman and sophomore years I was ridiculously shy. I got nervous if people looked at me in eyes, and I started to stutter and look away from 'em. I had this nervous habit of rubbing my head while talking to people, which made me look like I was bout to rob my interviewer. It was just a whole ass mess. So the interview continued and she asked me a question that I've never heard, "If you could compare yourself to a cartoon character, who would you choose and why?" Without thinking, I immediately said the Hulk.

(._.)

....
....

"Cause I wouldn't like you when you're angry?"

I couldn't even think of a good lie so I just said "YUP!" And started preparing myself to take this L.

Then the end of the interview came, and she told me everything I did wrong. Obviously the Hulk was the first thing she brought up. Then my eye contact. Then rubbing my head. Then she said, "I don't know if you've been taught this, but you should always wear a suit to an interview." Teddy B broke at this point, so if you not blessing the closet, be satisfied with this shirt and tie ensemble that I was sporting. Bitch, I was dapper. Then, the worst part happened.

Most of the L's I was prepared for, but this one completely blindsided me.

"Oh. And the shirt." She reached over to pull on it. "Is this a new style or is it on inside out?"

Exasperated sigh. Sure enough, my shirt was on inside out. HOW IN THE ACTUAL F*CK?! How did I button that shit?! And as if I didn't feel shitty enough, she criticized the hell outta my resume. And I left with my tail in between my legs.

Fast forward two years and a bunch of gained confidence later.

I saw a posting for an interview, and I noticed that it would be the same lady, so I put on my A++ game. Walked in that bitch with a three-piece suit on, with a name that I couldn't even think about pronouncing. Beard looking like something only Motions haircare could produce. Breath smelling like gold and success. Resume like the lost treasures of Atlantis. Smile like cocaine and Crest. I was on my shit.

Looked her in the eyes. Said every got damn thing with confidence. Then she asked me the SAME cartoon character question and what did I say? The Hulk. Then she looked at me and was like, "OOHH EYE REMEMBER YOU!!"

But WAIT!!! THERE'S MORE!!

"People look at me and think that because I don't smile much or because I'm quiet that I may be mean or mad, but in actuality, I'm a genuinely nice person. The Hulk smashes, but he also saves people." Smile.

Did I reach??? Arguably. Did I achieve?? Hell yea. If you listened closely, you could hear her draws get moist. She told me how great I did, then I later got offered an internship.

Ma'am. F*CK YO INTERNSHIP. I already had an offer from one I really wanted. I just did this to show you Teddy B dat dude. Not my exact words.

But yea. If this story had to have a moral it'd be that you live and you learn. Take each mistake as a lesson, and never make that same mistake again. Cliché quote here, cliché quote there.

If You Can't Laugh At Yourself (Two-fer)

I like to pick on folk. That's nothing new. I can also laugh at myself when things happen to me. I'ma break y'all off with a couple stories that weren't funny when they happened. Well to me, they weren't funny. But now I sit back and release a mighty guffaw when I reminisce.

I was at IHOP with my roommate Smelllroy and our two female neighbors that we weren't against knocking timberlands with, Drosario Dawson and Cameron D. Azz.

I had just finished crushing some country fried steak and cheese grits, and was ready to go back to the crib and be Nig Van Winkle. Right before we get ready to leave, it starts raining. And this is that Central Florida rain, so it's no light drizzle. Florida rain is ruthless for no damn reason. Me, a tourist, like the other millions have to ask, "Is a hurricane coming?"

Of course Drosario and Cameron D. ain't wanna go outside and get their hair wet, so I had to run to the car and pull it up. I was in my typical country boy attire. White T, basketball shorts, and house shoes. I went out the restaurant and ran to the car. Man on a mission. I ran cross the grass to get to my car. I stopped. Well, I tried. House shoes don't have traction on 'em. So I slid a good five feet before I finally wound up on my back. Feet straight up in the air. Diaper change swag. I was watching the rain fall on my face n shit. What is life?

I liked to think I immediately jumped up, but real shit, that whole debacle probably took a good long ass 45 seconds. I told myself that no one saw it, so I just got in the car. I looked in the subway across the lot, and employees and customers all in that bitch laughing at my ass. I mean, they obnoxiously fell out. One dude behind the counter took his shirt off and threw a tray of bread on the floor. Like you never seen someone slip before. Dickhead.

I ain't even go to that plaza anymore after that. Concentrated embarrassment. If I went back to Orlando tomorrow, I wouldn't go to that plaza cause there's always that one Subway employee that's been working there for 10+ years, and he probably would remember my ass.

I told Drosario and Cam what happened, and when I pulled off they're like, "Look they're still laughing!"

Get out my car heffas.

And now for your main event. Cue drumroll.

The Dizzney Free Ball!

It was my absolute last day working for the Mouse. My family was in town to help me pack and take me home. Before my shift, we all went to the parks. We went to the park I worked at last, so I could just walk to work and clock in. Simple right?

It's never simple with me. Never.

So the whole time I was walking to work, I got the urge to urinate. It's not helping that folk was running round playing in the fountains.

I was running late though, and I couldn't be late on my last day. So I planned this out. I was gonna break into a nice power walk so that I could get there in time, clock in, and then channel the Roman hood god of the sea Nep-goon and use the bathroom.

I finally reached my destination and this urine was BEYOND REAL! Like the pressure was on. I couldn't be a minute late, so I went to clock in first. While clocking in, I couldn't get my password right cause I was focusing on not peeing on myself. I was standing at the computer hitting the heel toe, tryna hold it in. I finally got the password right, and I was hustling down the hallway to the bathroom. I got to the door, and there's a guy that's coming out. We started doing that annoying ill-timed shuffle, where you go one way attempting to get out someone's way and they go the same direction. And then y'all go back and forth. Well, my bladder had its middle finger up right now, so I wasn't there for anyone's shit. "Heh, shall we dan-"

"OUT MY WAY!" Shove, then swim move.

I was determined to make it to that stall. I was on my last leg. I was panicking so much that I couldn't really focus on getting my zipper down. Like when you try to put the key in the lock so you can get in the house and go pee. I was losing it.

F*ck it! Just drop your shorts. Then... no.
Lawd Geezus NO!I CANT BELIEVE THIIIIISSSSS NOOOOOOOOOOOOOOOOOOOOOO!!!!

In my rush to pull my showts down, I prematurely summoned Nep-goon.

My draws were done – without a question. I threw 'em in the garbage and forgot they existed. I ain't smelling like a pamper for six hours. But, what was EYE to do?? I was already late getting to my shift. I needed to make a decision. Some would call it quits. You must remember that you always find a way. When HE closes a door, a window opens.

You've never quit. You're brilliant. NO ONE can keep you down. YOU'RE AN EFFIN SOLDIER!!!

I free balled. *It's only a 6 hour shift,* thought Teddy.

The weather is gorgeous, thought Teddy.

It started to rain. That Florida R&B video rain. This was why I know God has a sense of humor.

Lemme describe my uniform to you. A button up with various flags on it (freeeessshhh) and white shorts. WHITE. SHORTS.

I was good. I worked outside. But it's covered on top.

So I just posted up in the corner to avoid the rain. My coworker asked why I was acting funny and won't move. I told her. She tried not to die.

Remember that good ole sense of humor that God has? It started raining sideways. Unavoidable rain. I was hurt. I was tryna hide behind any objects, but this rain was very nonfictional. It was still hitting me. My coworker whistled at me and busted out laughing. And I already knew why.

"I'm out, ain't I?"

"Yep."

"My whole ass?"

"Your whoooole ass, hun. Beans and franks too."

Once my shift was over, I went RIGHT back into the street clothes. I'm a legend. I'm unforgettable.

The Hall Pass

Before I worked at Dizzney, I expected it to be like the most Magical thing in the world. Like every time you clock in, you're showered with confetti. If you get a great customer review, you get a Princess lap dance. You get to turn up with characters after work. Of course, it was nothing like that. The closest thing to magic I got was, "Hey Teddy, there's hot dogs in the break room. WITH chili." **Praise Break**.

But, BUUUTTT... There was this one magical time, we were given a hall pass. The managers wanted to do something special for all the interns cause our programs was almost over. So they took us to the Kagic Mingdom, and we had to break up into teams and do a scavenger hunt. Winners got movie passes. Whaaattt? We got paid to roam the park, and we didn't have to act like Carlton Banks while we do it?! I was all for it.

Well, before I get into this story, I wanted to talk about something hilarious that happened that day, but really has nothing to do with the story. There was this chick that worked in the same area as me. She was pretty stuck up. Drove an Escalade, kept a Gucci bag. She was one of them. She rarely came to work. She actually missed the day that they told us to come in for the scavenger hunt, but she somehow made it to the scavenger hunt. She rolled up with this big ass smile on her face, and the managers started looking at each other awkwardly while subtlety playing the nose game. The manager that lost had the pleasure of taking her around the corner and firing her right before we left.

So back to the story. We were a bunch of overworked college kids who had to bite their tongues when dealing with a massive amount of idiots every day. But being able to go to an actual park, in plain clothes around people that had NOOO clue you worked for the Mouse, and not have to answer questions like, "What time does the 9 o'clock fireworks start?" Bruuuuhhhh. Or, "How do I get to the monorail?" Idk cuh. It might be under that big ass sign that says "Monorail." And, "Is the main street parade on main street?" Stop it.

So being able to walk around the park knowing that the Mouse wasn't watching you AND getting paid to do it was an interns dream come true.

Lemme introduce my team:

Bobby D. From the Popeyes story.

James Stanko. My alabaster homie from Florida. Clowned around more than I did, so when we were together, foolishness ensued.

And Fail DeBarge. My bro from Mississippi, typically a model citizen, but I've witnessed him get pretty damn ignant.

So we're on our way to Kagic Mingdom, and if you've ever been to Dizzney world, and you've park hopped, you know that you can take the monorail to KM or you can take a boat. Stanko said we should just take the boat cause the monorail just left with some folk, and we can't let them get that big of a head start on us. And they both take the same amount of time. I didn't pay attention to that last part until later.

So we sitting on this boat, that's going slow as hell, and I was getting annoyed. So I decided to let it be known. "Stanko... why the hell did you think that this would get us there as fast as the monorail?"

"They told me it was the same speed."

"Bruh?? You believed that?! Why you let them insult you like that?" "What you mean?"

"This is a f*ckin BOAT. The monorail is a TRAIN. Don't let them lie to you and tell you that a got damn ferry boat is faster than a train!" At this point, I was starting to get attention from other guests and a couple of 'em felt the same as me. Unfortunately, they also finished drinking round the world at PEPCOT. So things decided to go left. Like far west.

Random inebriated eggshell colored gentleman said, "HELL YEA! THAT FUGGIN MOUSE HAS BEEN RAPING MY POCKETS SINCE TUESDAY. I SAY WE RAPE HIM!!!"

".... Oh..."

IMMEDIATE silence.

Smile removed from my face and the face of others. I sat right on down, put my headphones in, listened to some Neo Soul to calm down, and prayed for forgiveness for essentially inspiring the violation of a lovable childhood character. And my boss.

We finally finished the longest boat ride ever, and we're in Kagic Mingdom ready to win these movie passes and get ignant. As far as the scavenger hunt went, me, Stanko, Fail, and Bobby were killing it. We running through this hunt like it's nothing. Next up, we needed a picture with Lilo.

Well, while we looked for her, I saw my dog, my folk, my cuh cuh, my boy Pinokeeyo. I HAD to get a picture with him first. And to make things better, his character attendant was BEAUTIFUL! Well, to me she was. I like girls who are kinda funny looking. Big eyes, a crooked tooth, nose not aligned, stuff like that. So, she took a pic, and I started spitting that killa. "So I met 2Chainz and asked if he would take a picture with me. While posing, my sweater got snagged on his diamond chain. I yanked my sweater away, and his diamond necklace broke. How hard did I yank my sweater? Hard enough to break the ice. Hey beautiful, my name's Teddy, may I have your number?"

Of course she laughed. Who wouldn't? And she had an ugly ass laugh too, that's how I knew it was real cause she released that beast in public. Then this happened. I said, "Question, do you know where I can find Lilo?"

She replied, "Lilo?"

"Yea, we're doing a scavenger hunt, and I need a picture with her."

"Oh… so THAT'S why you talking to me? I knew it was something bout you." She sucked **hella teeth**. "I gotta take Pinokeeyo inside, bye!"

She walked away into the employee section.

"Wait, what?" I walked into the employee section after her cause I got my ID. "No, I talked to you cause I wanted your number. I just asked you a question cause I figured you'd know. Two birds, one stone." Then, BAM!!!! Punk ass Pinokeeyo headbutted the shit outta me. His nose got me RIGHT in my eye. I got an abundance of tears running down my right eye n shit. I WASN'T CRYING DOE.

My eye just sensitive.

Did I fight back? Nope, for a number of reasons. I didn't wanna be that dude that fought Dizzney mascots. And nine times outta ten, those short mascots are either a 4'11 Latino dude or a female. I didn't want to risk it. I took my L. I went back to the crew. Bobby asked, "Why you crying?" Snickers.

"I ain't crying. You know this Florida weather got my allergies all crazy."

Fail said, "NIGGA WE JUST SEEN YOU GET POKED BY PINOCH! DON'T PLAY IT OFF!!"

So, I dealt with that. For a while. I finally got them to focus on finishing this scavenger hunt. We found Lilo, took the picture, and had time to spare. So we went to be fat and indulged in those Pterodactyl legs they call turkey and some funnel cakes.

There was this dude there that Stanko HAAATED. I'd seen him around the apartment complex, and all he did was freestyle and breakdance. I mean, super douche. Ed Hardy to the socks. So let's call him Steve Douchemi. Anyways, apparently Douchemi cockblocked Stanko at a party, and he was still upset about it. So while Douchemi was freestyling, again, who know about what, Stanko tied his bookbag to the chair he was sitting in. While it was on his back. While he was sitting down. Smoove shit.

Well not so smoove, cause security seen him. Dude came up to Stanko. And I saw him, but I couldn't think of a way to warn him, but worst case scenario, they just tell him to untie the bag so it wouldn't too bad. But you know how shit goes when I'm involved. It never goes as planned. It goes left. Always.

Security sneaked up and yelled, "WHAT YOU DOING THERE YOUNG MAN?!" Ridiculously loud.

Stanko jumped up. Douchemi tried to jump up, but the chair was heavy and snatched him back. He flipped over the chair backward, and he was stuck, which is a hilarious sight. But he let out this dying giraffe noise, and I think he landed wrong and may have slightly injured himself. We all knew that we should probably get the hell outta there.

So we took off. And I was OOUUTTTT. I'm fast for a BigNig. I'm not like 4.4 40 fast, but I got some speed. That day I easily ran a 4.9 40.

Bobby yelled, "YO, GO TO THE MONORAIL!"

Nobody even looked back to see if security was after us, but we all knew that if we got caught, we could possibly get fired, and have to go back home and explain that we straight up got fired for running like Craig and DayDay through a Dizzney park.

Completely off topic, but there was this dude who got fired that worked in the same park as us, and he was SO SCARED to go home to his parents that he got a job at Wal-Mart and slept on various couches until his program was over. The struggle to fight the embarrassment was so real, and I didn't wanna experience it.

So yea. My big ass made it to the monorail, and I spread out on the chair and died a couple times.

We made it back and met up with our group. They checked our pages, and we got it all right.

Boss Man said, "Who was in your group?"

I said, "Me, Stanko, Bobby, and Fail."

"Aaaahhhh... sorry."

"What?"

"The ONE rule I gave was that you couldn't have more than three people on your team. So you're disqualified."

So basically, I got a sexual assault hit put on Miggey (which is still on my conscious cause I don't know if they followed through), got sonned by Pinokeeyo, and lost half a lung running from someone who probably wasn't chasing me. And I had nothing to show for it. Cool.

So yea. That was an eventful waste of my time.

120 Hours

Senior year of college was a combination of, "Ok you almost there, finish strong!" and, "What achievements must be made to get an honorary bachelor's degree? Do they give those out? Doctorates would be cool, but I ain't asking for much. I'm just tide boss." So they hired this new professor. He was from the Bahamas and got his PhD from one of those bougie ass schools. The man wanted a paper and presentation for just about every damn thing we discussed, and at the time, I just wasn't mentally prepared to be the student he wanted me to be in order to get a BET original movie made about his life.

Nothing was gonna be good enough for this guy. Let's call him Ho Clark. Sorry, I can't be more creative at the moment.

So I struggled through the whole semester. Towards the end, I took it upon myself to give me a day off from his class. And I also took it upon myself to put my foot in my own ass cause the day I missed was the same day this man decided to have everyone pick their groups for the final projects, and whoever was not in class that day or did not get chosen was in a group together.

So it was me, the sixth year senior, the dude who always came to class with a red eyed hangover, and the guy who was a lil slower than everyone else, but always received a pat on the back for his efforts.

And to add insult to injury, when I came to class the next day, he was reading off the list of groups, and I was hoping that the guy who I thought was my homie, Durty Vert ~~from my previous blogs~~, would've looked out for me and added me to his group. But he played me. So he read off all the groups and then said, "And the last group, that I put together due to absences arrrrreeee..."

A collection of shit eating grins immediately turned my way. I sat there and looked at the ceiling, ready to accept my fate. I was in the group with (in order of their descriptions above), Boris Hellnoe, Taye Niggs, and Aubrey FLAKE Graham (boy had immaculate dandruff).

The first part of the project was to open a restaurant in the next town over, research the target market including wants and needs. And some other BS.

The name of the town is Colonial Heights. We interviewed the manager of the local McDonald's who was not ashamed to be black and let us know, "I'm the manager of a McDonalds in the whitest damn town around. Why the hell you think they call it Colonial Whites?"

That's real. I appreciated it.

So me and Taye were in the library putting together a presentation about this struggleraunt we finna open. Boris and Flake were off... being off.

We're brainstorming on the project, bouncing ideas. He was a pro at photo editing, so he was gonna make the logo and such. I was writing everything out. His phone went off. Taye looked at his phone. "Uh oh, cheeeba cheeebaa!" "You tryna smoke now? Ween finish nothing!" "Look bruh, just write the intro. I'll take care of everything else. I gotta go."

And like a sucka, I believed him.

So we're in class. I was ready for him to tell me he had nothing, and we gotta wing it. But he had it! So we went up there ready to present.

I introduced myself to the class, he uploaded the power point, my back is facing the screen.

"My name is Mr. Belafonte and these are my team mates. We were given the task of opening a restaurant in Colonial Heights. We had to research the population and target market and we found that locally, people refer to it as Colonial Whites because of the population." I looked at the screen. This man had an American flag, and the background was some damn trailer parks and pickup trucks as the logo. And the words on the backdrop said, "Colonial Whites, we'll get ya right!"

And this...nigga, named the restaurant Colonial Whites. He will now take over while I go cry about something other than this project.

I'm not 100% sure about how the whole presentation went because once I saw the professors face frown up at the sight of the logo. I closed my eyes and kept singing ,"Rain On Me," by Ashanti as I went down with this ship. I do remember him going over the menu and I heard, "We have corn dogs cause white people love corn dogs".

RAAAIIIIINN OOOONNN MEEE.
LLLAAAAAWWWWWDDD WON'T YOU TAKE
THIS PAIN FROM MEEEEEEEE.

When I opened my eyes, this fool had the nerve to say, "Any questions or comments?"

BRUUUUUUHHHHH.

The way Dr. Clark repeatedly called us ignorant, I just felt like I was standing in front, blindfolded, and the whole classroom got guns. So Professor Clark gave us the second part of our project that's like, 800% of our final grade. We had to pick a state, pick a hotel for accommodations to meet the needs of sports fans. I think. I still don't know. I remember we chose Texas for whatever reason.

I stayed up all night writing a rough draft of everything I think this man needs just to see if I was on the right track. I put my heart into this draft. I made a whole pot of coffee, put it on ice, chugged it, booboo'd my life away, and went to class. I showed him what I had so far. "No, no, no. Mr. Belafonte this is all wrong. You need to figure out your market, interests, average age, likes dislikes, wants, state birds, fruit, dropout rate, and Bun B's social security number." *Do I really need a degree?*

So I went to the rest of my classes, met with the group, tell them everything he wanted, and assigned topics. 48 hours. No sleep.

I went back home to rewrite it on top of everything else I had to do for school. Make another pot of coffee, chugged it, booboo'd my life away, went to my 8 am Bio class. I walked in at 8:10 and all the desks were spread out. Why are they spread out? cause this was the final exam. And the only thing I knew was Bun B's social security number, and that the nucleus was the control center of the cell.

I was pretty sure I'ma let Dr. Clark down, and I couldn't bomb two classes, so I lemme sit in the back, pull my phone out, and see if Google can give me a B. So while I was cheating my ass off, my stomach felt crazy. It wasn't like I gotta use the bathroom. Pain, it was just a pain. So I asked my bio professor if caffeine had an effect on your stomach.

"Oh yea, it eats away at the lining your stomach."

Safe to say I had no lining on my stomach. Stomach just raw dogging the rest of my digestive system.

Later, I showed Professor Clark what I had so far.

"You're kinda getting there. You need Dirk Nowitzki's 3 point average in elementary school, and Jerry Jones' lineage, and some other things, but keep going." *I WILL be a statistic.*

Flake came over my house to write his part. He fell asleep halfway through while I was shorting out my computer by crying tears into my keyboard.

Made another pot of coffee cause, to hell with my stomach lining. Chugged it. Peed Folgers. Went to class. 72 Hours. No sleep.

By this time, I was hallucinating. I saw monkeys run across the interstate on my way to class. I tried to talk to someone and all I could do was mumble.
I met with Dr. Clark one more time, and when he asked me what my problem was, I couldn't speak because I had a lump in my throat.

"Mr.Belafonte, if you don't have anything to say I have a meeting to get to."

"I just... I don't..." Tears started flowing. "I don't know what you want. And I've wrote four pages every night, and it's not right. And I don't wanna be in college anymore cause of this project and they hiring at Food lion distribution. I don't know where those monkeys came from on 95 South, and the news ain't say anything about them missing, and now I'm sad cause they got unclaimed chimps in Petersburg."

"Mr. Belafonte, calm down. Get it together. I've seen you're dedicated, and it's admirable. Just tell me how many minutes Mike Jones used on his phone plan since he gave his phone number out, and you'll be on the right track. Now go to the restroom and clean yourself up."

I went and looked at myself in the bathroom mirror. *I still don't know shit.* Boo hoos.

Flake sent me his paper, so I went into the computer lab to look over it. Ain't a complete sentence in four pages. I was screaming into my hands, cussing his ass out. He's not there, I was just venting. This girl spoke up. "Teddy,you not right. Like I feel like you going in on him, you know how he is. Don't be mean." "I'm not being mean. I've been working with him about this, and all I want is a damn page of something correct. This man has an entire page of shit with red and green lines under them. Do you know what that means? That means that out of four pages, this man has one whole page, a quarter of his part, 250 words that a damn computer program can't understand. And he's ok with that shit, but I'M outta line?!" So I stayed up and fixed my paper, and drank another pot of coffee. Booboo'd coffee beans. And went to class. 96 Hours. No sleep.

I was actually very content with my life because I knew I would be admitted to an asylum before the paper was due so everything is ok. I didn't bother talking to Dr. Clark because at this point, f*ck him. The paper was due tomorrow, and we decided that he was gonna get whatever we had.

I went home, stayed up and wrote my paper and edited Flakes final draft. Drank a pot of coffee. Trimmed the coffee bean plant that was growing in my toilet bowl and headed to campus.

I turned the paper in and prayed that Dr. Clark either got fired or went back to the Bahamas for good. I slept for sixteen hours. The semester was over. Boris finally popped up and gave me a phone call.

"Aye bruh, guess what? Dr. Clark said our shit was so bad, he had no clue what anybody was talking about and couldn't find a grade low enough to give us so he gave us C's and quit."

That was cool with me. Class of 2011 HOE!

I Never Taught Folk To Fish

So my homie back home in North Carolina is a teacher at this small town high school. And he invited me to come speak at their Career day, mainly to talk as a college graduate. Me, not really having a career at the time, was hesitant to accept the offer, but was like, what the hell, let me drop some gems on these kids. Now, this school needed a whole army of black male coaches of an underprivileged, winless team in the hood, led by a white woman from the suburbs who would do whatever it took to get them to graduate, so she could rub it in her families' face. So the standards ain't that high round there.

So during the drive down, I was nervous! I was in the car more unprepared than my Grandma at a "Get off the couch without grunting" contest. Once I crossed state line, I was on my way into a panic attack because feces was finna become authentic. I could A, flake on the whole program, and drown myself in a pitcher of blue moon and bury myself in mounds of barbecue and slaw. B, do an EXTREMELY awkward Career day presentation with my bad ass nerves. Or C, I could swing through the Alphabet store and the gas station, and grab the nerve calmer and instant courage duo that is Newpoat 100's and Pepsennessy.

I arrived to the school smelling like your uncle, but I hid it pretty well, thanks to spearmint gum and

GREAT cologne. I ain't know what to expect, so I kept the half bottle of Pepsennessy in my back pocket just in case. I meet my homeboy, Jonah Trill, and he took me to his classroom full of hood hamsters and sperm goons (11th grade), and gave me the introduction. "Class, I'd like to introduce you to a good friend of mine, Teddy, who is going to speak to you about what lies ahead. He is a…"

HOLY SHIT I NEVER TOLD HIM WHAT I DID.

I was waiting tables at the time fresh out of college, but I couldn't show the kids my struggle.

"Well, I'ma let him explain it to you."

I stepped up to the podium, shaking. I took a big swig of the cleverly hidden CB, and my mouth just started moving. I started off professional.

"First off I'd like to thank you guys for having me. I'd like to start off with a question, if I may? How many of you guys have applied to college or another institute, or plan on applying between now and next year?" Classroom fifty deep, two people raise their hands. *Oops. Welp I can't talk about what to expect in college if they asses ain't going.*

The speech I attempted to write in my head is useless right now. You ever been in a position where being real trumps being professional? If you know what I'm saying. If not, hopefully this explains it.

"Soooo… y'all finna get jobs? Or nah?" A couple of chuckles. "Oh so y'all do hear me? Don't get me wrong, I'm not against going out and getting an honest job. I'm also a believer that college isn't for everyone. BUT education is."

Smart ass niglet, how that make sense? College ain't for everyone, but education is? That's like, a double negative bruh. If that's what college does for you, have you thinking like that, I definitely ain't going. Why are you stupid?

"If you go to a trade or vocational school, and educate yourself in a field, get hands on experience, and work your way up, you didn't attend college, but you've been educated. If you shadow and work under someone who owns a landscaping company, and learn the ropes, you didn't attend college, but you've been educated. May I continue or you wanna put 25 more cents in and try again?"

Boom. Random "ooooohhhsss" and a single "oh shit." Pepsennessy kicked in. I don't eeeeevvvveeennnn try to fight it cause I see these kids need something real to straighten they ass up cause I know they haven't gotten it yet. Hindsight, I should've chosen a better way to start off.

I looked over at JT with a look he'd only seen when we tipped the bottles. I was finna go on a drunken rant. I rubbed my forehead.

"Life." Sigh. "Life is finna hit y'all with some shhhiiiiiiiiiiiiiiiiiiiiiiit boy."

Students: O__O

JT's feyonce and the science teacher whispered, "Ummmm Teddy, that's not-"JT shushed her. "Shhh. He's going somewhere with it. I'm pretty sure."

"That's what life does. No matter who you are. Obstacles get thrown at you every day. Some of 'em you gone bunny hop over with ease, others, you gon stumble over them things. How you bounce back is what makes you YOU. When I was in college, there was a point where I thought I would've been with Pookie slap boxing for crack rocks because I couldn't see me finishing, and I couldn't see other options. But I got it together and came back fighting. That's resiliency. Fifty something folk in here and two said y'all applying to colleges. That's crazy. What's some of the reasons y'all not applying?"

Students replies included, "I don't wanna get rejected"and "I don't wanna flunk out," and something stupid I'll get to in a lil bit.

I wrote their examples on the board.

"First of, lemme start with THIS nugget." I pointed to the comment. "cause I don't know what he on. Bruh, you aren't applying to college cause your girl

119

has two years left of school to your one?! So what do you plan on doing after you graduate?"

"I'ma keep working at Finish Line until she graduate, and then I may follow her to school."

"And If you don't get in?"

"Probably just move up there to be close anyway."

"You threw it up, and it turned into sunshine, huh?"

"What??"

"Never mind. Look, that's shit. THAT'S why you won't apply to college???"

JT said, "He got a 3-something-GPA, so it won't be a problem getting into one." I whispered to myself, "Lawd, he's a smart dumbass."

"You follow your significant other to college. Your first screw up is that you're settling for less to make someone else happy. Then y'all see each other all the damn time, which gets old fast. You have no time to miss each other, and when y'all try to get space apart, you might hear some he say she say that you won't like. At the end of the day, where y'all gone be?? Not together, that's for damn sure. You find yourselves in college. Pretty damn hard to do that with someone up ya ass 24/7. And I'ma check in with JT every nine weeks next year to keep a foot in ya ass til you apply to college. cause I know you got the juice." Swig of CB. "And don't overthink everything right now to the point where you stress out and scare yourself out of doing it. I'm not saying don't give a damn about your grades, but don't be afraid of flunking out. cause you're gonna panic, and screw up your youthful hair lines. And probably run away from issues instead of knocking them bad boys out. That's no good. Put it like this: You write a paper, and all you concentrate on and stress is the conclusion and how you're gonna finish it, the paper itself ain't gon be shit. I'ma let that marinate." *Please marinate.*

"Look, I got real with y'all cause I wanna be that push. Y'all can do great things. I SEE THAT SHIT. Go out there, grind, suffer, persevere. Be strong and be successful. Do it for me, if not for anybody else. And maybe, JUST MAYBE, someone will direct a straight-to- TV movie about this moment right here. Love y'all." A standing hood chipmunk and spermgoon ovation. Was I misty eyed at this point??

Bitch I might be.

"Anybody have any questions for Teddy?"

A student asked, "So where did you wind up graduating from?" "I went to college with JT. Class of 2011." Another student asked, "So, what do you do?" "Ahhh mayyynneee. Funny you asked me that...It was nice speaking to y'all."

121

Was I inappropriate? At times. Did they hear me? Absolutely. JT said he got students asking him questions about college cause they wanna be like Teddy. Good thing they didn't know I was a struggling blogger. I'll return to the motivational speaking when I get some money on me.

Some People Sit Back And Watch The World Burn. My Coworkers Are The Ones Holding Matches And Kerosene

After I graduated college, I was still developing photos at your favorite drug store. I needed a come up. I needed to mature. I needed a big boy job. So I started waiting tables. I had the pleasure of slanging crab cakes at a lovely seafood restaurant. Let's call it "The Musty Krab." It was my first Christmas party at the Crab. I had never really partied with taupe folks for real, so this was all new.

I guess I'll start from the beginning of this f*ckery to give you an idea of the setting I was in. I went to my friend's house, which I affectionately refer to as the Space Invader, to pregame with brandy and cream soda. Which is f*ckin delicious by the way. A Goonsicle is what they call it.

Anywho, I was at the Space Invader's crib with the homie Wolvaqueen, his bro and her bf Leo DeFAPrio, and two other co-workers, Flionel Richie and Fletch Luger. We get our pregame on, but unfortunately we lost a soldier. Fletch Luger was called home by the Porcelain gods. Never pregame with rookies.

So I had to play taxi and scoop a couple folk to take to the party and I get there an hour late. I thought it started at eight, so I had to walk in a room full of white people on CP time.

Within the first few hours, I got my Pepsennessy on, taught a bunch of egg shell colored people how to wobble, then left them to fend for themselves. I straight murdered karaoke with some clueless teenagers, and broke up more fights in a night than I have in my whole life. I bet you wanna hear more about those fights, dontcha?

Well, towards the end of the night, I was (somewhat) sober in a room full of extremely inebriated taupe people. My boss, Bony Soprano, and his wife and my other boss, Blondatella Vosace, were giving their thank you speeches. And THIS was the beginning to shit gettin real. During the speech my manager, Kate Thinslet, said something quietly and her ex (whom she hates), Zack Slorris, felt the need to reply by yelling, "SHUT THE F*CK UP."

Me tryna look out, I pushed him out the way and got in between them. After the speech, Thinslet ran off somewhere and they formed a search party to look for her. Meanwhile, I was outside hanging with a Newpoat, and Zack came outside. Thinslet's friend, LeAnn Dimes, asked me what happened. I told her and another one of my coworkers' brothers, Ryan Gfest (there are ALOT of people involved in this story), overheard that Zack yelled at Thinslet. Then he, also drunk off his ass, replied, "YOU LIKE YELLIN AT GIRLS BRO?! F*CKIN YELL AT ME BRO!"

Then Zack's mini guido ass wanted to act like he'd bust a grape. So he started bouncing around talkin shit like, "OH COME AT ME! I'M 22, HOW OLD R U BRO HUH? TOO DAMN OLD TO BE TRYING TO FIGHT ME. SUCKS TO BE YOU!"

Keep in mind Gfest was a whole foot taller than Zack. I don't want these people to fight, I was cool with both of them, so I grabbed Zack and pushed him away. He was still tryna charge Gfest, so I just wrapped him up and told him I wouldn't let go until he calmed down. This guy channeled some kinda MMA shit and ducked down, spun around, picked a bale of hay, and pushed me to get to Ryan.

My inner negro came out. I'd been keeping it in for the eight months I'd worked there, but it made an appearance for three seconds. I shoved Zack, HARD, and said, "Push me again, bitch." That problem was solved. Then out of nowhere, Gfest disappeared, and an even drunker opponent appeared and tried to fight Zack. So I carried his ass in the restaurant.

I told the Chef (Zack's boss), who happened to be almost the same size as the guy on the label of my favorite canned goods and should've also been the main one outside trying to break shit up, about his workers outside. Out of nowhere, this bald bearded brother, who I initially assumed was an ally, ran up to me. "YO YOU GOT A PROLLEM WIT MY MAN?! "?????" "DON'T WALK UP ON MY

MANS LIKE THAT!" Ralph said, "Yo, it's cool. We're friends." "NAW I DON'T LIKE THE WAY HE TALKIN TO YOU!"

I said, "I…. I'm talkin like I'd talk to anyone else." Then Ralph chimed in, "He's cool, man. Just go back to the bar." "NAW BRO! BACK UP OFFA MY MAN." B&B walked away. The bad thing was, I didn't even realize my life was in danger until 75% of that conversation was done.

Meanwhile, another one of my wasted coworkers, Katie Brolmes, had just got proposed to by her equally wasted boyfriend. It went something like this: "Um, Katie, baby. I love you, babe. Will you marry me babe? Babe…"

Katie, with snot bubble sobs, nodded her head.

And what do drunk mf's do to celebrate an engagement??? THEY TAKE MORE SHOTS OF RUBBING ALCOHOL. I'ma come back to them.

So I went back outside, and I saw yet ANOTHER COWORKER, Lindsay Goham, and her boyfriend outside yelling at the top of their lungs. And she's like, 4'11 and 95 pounds, talking shit like she's economy sized. He was in people's faces, and she was ridiculously drunk screaming across the parking lot. "YOU GUYS ARE F*CKIN CHILDREN!! Y'all ARE PUNKS! F*CKIN BITCHES!! Oh my F*CKIN SHOE CAME OFF."

I just needed to get her to the car, so I threw her over my shoulder and put her in someone's car. Now we gotta get her boyfriend in the car, which was a more difficult task. So I calmly went up to him.

"Aye bruh, ya girl in the car. Go check on her so we can get y'all home."

"Now what?! You wanna fight me too?"

"You gotta be shittin me. Do I have 'I'm that nigga you wish would' written on my got damn forehead?"

While I was tryna get him to the car, Goham got out the muhf*cka. So one of the Spanish goon cooks, Fidel CasDro, who is cartel crazy and also just finished making out with a bottle of Tequila, called himself trying to calm Goham down by rubbing on her stomach. This pissed her boyfriend off.

"THAT'S ENOUGH OF THAT TOUCHING SHIT!" He shoved CasDro.

Big mistake. Why? cause not only was CasDro crazy, his ass was a packaged deal. You f*ck with him, you gotta f*ck with his boy 2STRIKEZ!! And he had the shortest temper in Central Virginia.

So one of my coworkers was trying to calm Goham and her boyfriend down. And I was trying to calm CasDro and 2STRIKEZ!! down. Goham's boyfriend got in the car, so I thought shit was cool. It was not.

Goham's ass got out the car and ran towards me. I still had no clue how the hell I pissed her off. She just told me she loved me literally five minutes before this shit, but I ain't notice her. Until she had my shirt collar and my cardigan in that pitbulls jaw she called a fist. Then her boyfriend tried to pick her up to get her off of me, but I'm like, "Um, bruh. She needs to let go first before you pick her up like that."

So now I was basically being hung by my own freshness cause she refused to let go and he refused to put her down. After thirty the longest seconds ever, she let go. Cardigan dangling off my shoulder, holding on for dear life. T-shirt for a capital U-Neck going on. Finally, finally, FINALLY they both got in the car and leave. My night was over. But of course it wasn't. The devil started moving through that party. When this occurred, I was almost sure the Mayans were right about that whole end of the world shit. Bald & Bearded crossed paths with 2STRIKEZ!! And it wasn't no, "Oh I stepped on your shoe, my bad, young brother," encounter.

2STRIKEZ!! and CasDro were upset, telling the boss Bony Soprano what had happened with Goham. Bald & Bearded saw that and thought 2STRIKEZ!! was threatening Bony. But see, I was sober when he approached me. My judgement was intact. 2STRIKEZ!!, on the other hand, was drunk and had not a mineral of f*cks left to give. And he saw B&B unbutton his shirt to reveal a wife beater and all hell broke loose. cause we all know, a wife beater is the universal signal for, "Square up." A clash of hood Titans is the only thing I can compare this to. If we didn't break them up, those dudes could've EASILY destroyed a small city.

The shit that tripped me out is that during all of these fights, the bar manager, TD Flakes, was outside smoking a cigarette. He was looking at us during each fight like, "Sheeiiitttt, these niggas think I'm wrinkling this suit, they got me ALL f*cked up." So we separated B&B and 2STRIKEZ so nothing else crazy happened. We tried to calm 2STRIKEZ!! down by forcing cigarettes down his throat. Bald & Bearded went away and everything was cool. Kinda. As B&B walked out to leave, I asked him if everything was good.

"Yea man we good. I'm just saying, I'm from Baltimore. I sell COKE!!" Then he walked off into the darkness. Damn fine exit. Damn fine.

After all this shit happened, I saw Thinslet, FINALLY. Didn't know where the hell she'd been, but I tried to console her and give her a hug. You know what this drunk broad did? First, stiff armed me. Second hit me with, "I don't feel like talking to ANYONE!" Last, twisted my wrist, cause apparently step one wasn't bad enough. I WAS SICK AND TIRED OF THESE MF'N BABY POWDER COLORED COWORKERS!

So back to the newly engaged drunks.

Katie Brolmes told me to go congratulate her new fiance cause he was feeling down. "Hey man, congrats on your engagement bro. I wish you much success." I stuck my hand out. Fiance hugged me.

"Thanks man. I love you bro."

"Aaalllllright. It's like our... second time seeing each other, but uhhhh... I guess if that's how you feel. (Awkward turtle) I love you too."

At least an hour passed, and if Katie Brolmes wasn't dancing, she was crying. Then she just fell out her damn chair. And THAT was when Bony decided it was her time to go. So he walked her to the parking lot. But here's the messed up thing. She was going towards the car, and her fiance just walked the hell off into the damn woods, like he was mad at the world. I ain't seen him since, but I'm assuming he made it home. Zack drove Katie home, and she puked in his car, so there's karma biting his ass.

As for me and my house, never drinking with taupe people again. "When white folk get drunk they ackaFOOL!! Black people drunk just wanna bang each other." – My Mama

Rage Quit in 5,4,3...

While at The Musty Krab, I developed a deep respect for servers. I also developed a feeling of guilt that I don't think I can ever redeem, because of all the 10% tips I've left. And the intoxicated dine and dashes I committed in college. Karma definitely kicked me in my ass during my serving career.

For a while, I worked Saturday mornings. Saturday mornings were a gift and a curse. It wasn't stressful, and you were out the door quick, but it was a guaranteed $40 shift cause it was so slow. I mean, who wakes up like, "Maaayynne, I could really go for some crabcakes"? Twelve people do. So there was only three servers and a manager on the floor, and the servers rotate and bus their own tables until dinner shift folk come through. Simple enough, right? Well this one particular Saturday, which happened to be the beginning of Black History Month, separated the men from the boys.

You remember the Christmas party story, right? You just read it! I talked about my coworkers, Kate Thinslet, and my engaged coworkers LeAnne Dimes and Chadam Vinatieri. Well, we were all together on this day. It started out a normal Saturday. Clean and set up and watch that one old couple sit outside until we opened. Once we opened, we all had our rotations going on. Ain't but six people in the restaurant. 1:30 hits, and the kitchen staff went on break. Three cooks went to the gym, two cooks and a dishwasher hold it down. SOOOOOOOOON as they leave, folk started coming in the door. It started picking up, but ain't nothing we hadn't done before. I did my normal walk around to check the whiteboard to see what table I got next. I got a couple, no biggie. I just had to stop being Saturday lazy and take it up a notch.

I went in the back to make some drinks, and picked up some food. I came back to the front, and it was Black Friday out this bitch. I checked my list, and I got two four tops and one nine top. For non servers, it's how many people are at the table.

So I hit my go to. Take everybody's drink orders. Serve that ass. Take food orders. Serve that ass. No time for conversations today folks. Hot food and cold drinks are all I had to give.

Throughout all the mayhem, I kept walking round and saw this table full of black people just looking around sad as hell. Every time I passed by, they were more irritated. On a regular day, I would've just taken their order until their server had time to get to them. BUT THAT DAY? Ain't no time.

I did another round, and Kate came up to me like, "Teddy did you get that 9 top?"

"Yes I did."

"Did you get that OTHER 9 top?"

Cue record scratch. Get the hell out my face. What other nine top? Bruh, my soul pop locked outta my body. I just KNEW it was that table full of annoyed black folk I had been Instagram model curving since they sat down. They finna unload on my ass.

Sure enough it was. Only thing to do now is what my OG server taught me. "Y'all look thirsty."

Brought nine glasses of water to the table. I apologized to them, and began to take their order. Then one of my tables was waving frantically for my attention. I went over there.

"My clam chowder tastes off."

Well got dammit, turn it on, I ain't got time. I'm only giving cold drinks and hot food. YOU should've prepared your taste buds for off chowder. I went in the back to try and attempt to turn these folks frowns upside down. My composure was strong, though. In this situation, I looked to Kate Thinslet cause if she strong, I was strong.

Chadam was off in the cut in the midst of a level 5 meltdown. He picked up his plate and puts it back down. *Welp! Don't have time for that!* He filled a cup half way, and slammed it back down. *Don't have time for that shit either!* He picked up the silverware. *Absolutely no time for that.* Just making everyone around him nervous as hell.

THE WHOLE KITCHEN FORGOT HOW TO KITCHEN!

You got dishwashers making salads and desserts. Running food out to tables and shit. I was so certain we were gonna go out of business that day. I looked to Kate for that motivation I needed to finish strong.

And it was nowhere to be found.

She was at the soda machine, making drinks and crying her spirit out. "Teddy, I don't know what to do. I DON'T KNOW WHAT TO DO!!!"

First order of business was to stop crying. One, cause you're better than that and I need you with me right now and two, you crying into their drinks. Sierra Mist finna be salty as hell.

Bruh, you know what made things worse? LeAnne Dimes was CHILLING. Completely worry free. She was walking round, getting all her orders to her tables effortlessly, whistling and shit. Making all of us look unstable and incapable of doing or jobs. Then she got the nerve to say, "It's getting a little busy isn't it?"

Girl, shut up!
I should whoop yo ass for being so calm.

Kate Thinslet had to make an executive decision, because we was bout to drown. She called Trillary

Tuff, who was working dinner shift, and asked if she could come in early cause we was finna be Tumbleweed Town in thirty minutes. She said she'd be there as fast as she could.

Then she called my homie, Slim Carrey, and asked if he could come in and bus tables. He let her know he was fresh outta driving school and didn't have time to stop home. She ain't care. We needed whatever we could get. My boy was outchea bussing tables in an Adidas tracksuit. EFFORTLESSLY might I add.

Trillary Tuff called the restaurant while digging in her husband's ass because he was driving. "I'm coming as fast as I can. ROBBIE DRIVE FASTER!!!" She got there and started getting it done. I mean, she got her husband in a white tee and jeans taking folks drink orders! WE STRONG!!!

I could see the light at the end of the tunnel. I may not have to quit after all. My tables were not satisfied in the least bit, but f*ck it, they ate.

Then the cavalry arrives. The dinner shift. I survived!

When the shift was over, I rewarded myself with the biggest Ribeye steak we had in the joint, and a Blue Moon. The manager told me I ain't have to pay cause she just KNEW I was gonna quit. Ya boy did it.

F*ck that day though.

Of Mice & Teddy

We all know life tests us. In my head, I think life knows that there are certain situations you haven't been through in a while, if ever. And it wants to know if you sink or swim. Life is the teacher that called on you because she KNOWS that you don't know the order of operations. So you either get the answer right, or you blurt out "SOHCAHTOA."

The choice is yours.

This particular time, life just decided to make eight hours of my life painfully awkward to see if I had it. I'll let y'all be the judge of whether I did or not.

I was waiting tables at the Musty Krab, and I was the only non-taupe server in the restaurant. It was 3 p.m. on a Saturday, so it was pretty slow. Me and my homie Slim Carrey were in the back cutting up, horse playing. You know, shit we ain't have no business doing. There's this taupe girl we worked with. Bout 5'0 , 100 pounds soaking wet. One of those innocent girls obsessed with horses. So let's call her Pony Montana. Me and Slim got in a friendly shoving contest. I pushed him the exact moment as Pony came walking our way. He flew towards her, his shoulder hitting her in the nose.

The nose is a very interesting body part. Because if you get hit in it, you either sneeze violently, or you're in excruciating pain.

Now I was in a situation similar to when you hit your younger sibling, and you pray they're okay because you don't want them to tell mom. Except lil brother= tiny taupe girl, and mom= County PD.

So I went to hug her to make sure she's okay, and I couldn't see her face, but the way her body was moving, she was either crying or laughing. I prayed for the latter, but y'all know my luck. She started boo-hooing. Everybody in the kitchen gave me death stares. Slim screamed, "LOOK WHAT YOU DID!" and her boyfriend was mad at me, but he can't whoop my ass. So he probably slid a racial slur in under his breath while he was checking on her.

I apologized, but she was not trying to hear it, so I felt small at this point. There wasn't but five people in the back, but when I went to the front, everybody knew what happened. And I was public enemy #1.

My manager, Kate Thinslet, gave me some words of encouragement, you know, "It was an accident. People know you're a good guy, and you didn't mean it." So now I was ready to work. I still felt bad, but I just tried to find stuff to do to get my mind off it. I had to clean the fish tank before the dinner rush. This fish tank was huge, almost to the point where they should sell tickets for folks to look at it. It had these heavy thick wooden doors on the bottom of it. You had to get on a step stool to clean it, so while I was climbing down, my apron got caught on one of the heavy ass doors which happened to be off the hinges. It fell and made this loud obnoxious ass noise.

When I turned around, all these egg shell colored folk are looking at me like I just said I'd never seen Titanic. Which I haven't by the way. I looked to the right, and Kate had her hand over her mouth and tears falling from her eyes. cause of course, my day couldn't get more awkward with the heavy ass door that I knocked over landing on her foot the same day she decided to be cute and wear sandals.

So I carried her, princess style to the back. She was crying her ass off. The other managers were in the back with me, and she decided she wanted to win a f*ckin Oscar, so she's like, "My FOOOOOOTTTT!! I CAN'T FEEL ANYTHING, IT'S NUMB!! I KNOW IT'S BROKEN!!"

So I got more death stares. The owner, Bony Soprano, took her to the clinic, and I continued my shift feeling so microscopic while everyone prepared to burn a Teddy effigy. Bony called and asked to speak with me. "Aye man, don't feel bad. She didn't break anything. It's just swollen and she's fine and she can walk." Ok. So I didn't feel that terrible anymore. I could keep my head in the game.

No I couldn't.

Because a few hours later, in comes Kate, again, working on that Oscar. On crutches, foot wrapped up, making unnecessary ass grunts. Folk start joking like, "Look what you did Teddy. I hope you're proud." I felt so bad I couldn't even look her crippled ass in the face. I felt like John Coffey. Minus the... you know.

I felt like Lennie from Mice and Men, breaking taupe girl's necks and shit. Tell me about the rabbits, bruh.

Stages of Fade Grief

My most recent job was at a high school. It was fun for the most part, because you think about how crazy these kids are, and you SWEAR you weren't like that in high school but you were. You totally were.

One day I was doing lunch duty, and a teacher came up to me, and said another staff member was holding a kid back in the lunch line and looked like he needed help. This school was so well behaved there was NEVER any action, so I was all for it. I went over there, and it was my homeboy holding a student back, but he said the student calmed down so he let him go. The student had not, in fact, calmed down, because he went back to the student and got in his face. Now the student that my boy was holding back was bigger. He wasn't fat, but he was built like Cole from Martin, so I'll call him Thic Flair. The dude he was going after was smaller but I'd seen him play football, and he was scrappy so I had no clue how stuff would go down.

So Flair gets back in dudes face, and they talking trash, but lil bruh said he ain't want no problems. Well Flair decided that he wanted some problems that day. Flair pushed him, and lil bruh decided that this was NOT finna be a shoving contest, and called what I like to refer to as, "The Hands audible." Lil bruh just started throwing them things. Quick too. Flair tried to throw some haymakers, but whenever he cocked back, Dwyane Fade already tagged him twice, so Flair missed every punch he threw. The lunch lady was screaming, slamming her hands on the bar, going ham. Mashed potatoes and gravy flying everywhere. Me and my boy ran over to break it up, and of course, he walked outta the cafeteria with the winner. I had to pick Flair ass up off the floor. He leaning all on me like Jordan when he finished the Flu Game. In my head I'm like, *Damn bruh he ain't give you no body shots why you limping?* He was holding his eye like, *Nahh my eye. It just swell up real easy.*

I took him to the office to seal his fate.

Me and my boy got back in line and the lunch lady was like, "I... I just didn't know what to do, so I started banging and screaming to get someone's attention for help." We was right there though.

Another male staff, who walked over there with me and straight disappeared once the fight broke out, was like, "Yea, Mr. Such and such has a few inches on me, so I felt he was better equipped to handle it." You taller than me though.

Flair got suspended for ten days and after his suspension, I was curious about how he was gonna handle his return, and all the Q&A that came with it. So I kept a close eye on him. I took the ONE required psychology class in college, so I was very well educated on the stages of fade grief.

One, denial. I was standing in the hallway in between classes, and another student went up to Flair like,"Where you been, bruh?"

"I got suspended."

"Damn, bruh. What you do?"

Flair shook his head, and walked off into a crowd. Flair class wasn't even in that direction. He just didn't wanna relive those moments. I ain't messy, so I couldn't scream out, "OH HE GOT SOAKED IN THE LUNCH LINE, LIKE SOME DAY-OLD DIRTY DISHES!"

Flair was in denial. And who was I to give him a reality check?

Two, anger. Bruh was just mad at everybody who wasn't D. Fade. He felt like he needed a W. And anybody could get fired on. Except for D. Fade. I later found out that Flair was a nineteen-year-old freshman, and D. Fade was fifteen or sixteen. So getting rinsed by someone who can't technically see a Rated R movie without his mama, while you outchea buying cigarettes and lottery tickets, was arguably frustrating. Three, bargaining. Bruh was def heard saying, "Man I swear on everything I love, if I ever see that nigga outside of school, I'ma get mine." This wasn't one of those fights up for debate. It was obvious he was outmatched. But who was I to tell bruh, "All fades matter?"

Four, depression. This one stuck out to me like a white woman at Essence Fest. I stood behind bruh in the SAME lunch line he caught the fade in. He leaned against the wall, shoulders all slumped over. Got his hoodie on and tied tight. Normally I was supposed to tell him to pull his hood down but this kinda fade was probably the worst bad hair day you could have.

Ba dum tsssss.

Unfortunately, we didn't reach the acceptance stage. He was a lil young, so it mv take a while, if ever. I never got a chance to talk to him cause he never returned after spring break. But I wanted to let him know, there IS life after fades.

Teddy B A Daddy

So, sometime in September of 2013, while my dating game was at peak strength, I met this young lady. We went on a few dates, then decided to make things official. She became Booski. Typical love story, you know how it goes:

Teddy & Booski sittin in a tree,
K-I-S-S-I-N-G.
First comes love,
Then comes requests,
Then comes Teddy buying pregnancy tests.

Something like that.

Anywho, my life began to change about seven or eight months later. Then the big day arrived.

It all started at about 2 a.m. on February 19, 2015. I woke up, and Booski told me she was having some nonfictional ass contractions. Me being the supportive partner that I am...I panicked my ass off.

She told me to calm down, cause they're not consistent. I couldn't sleep, so I just played Xbox and monitored her until I had to go to work. I asked if I needed to call out and tend to her, and she goes, "No. cause you're gonna get on my nerves and panic. I'm going to work."

HHHWWWWWHHHYYYYY are you going to work?!

"Fool this is not a movie. I'm not gonna crown in the car. I'm good. Go to work."

I got to work and I couldn't even sit down. I was so nervous. I just paced back and forth around the office, like one of those shooting gallery ducks.

Work was terribly slow which did not help. I finally got busy at work towards the end of my shift, and she called twice. When I finally got a chance to answer the phone, "Soooo, don't panic, but my contractions are ten minutes apart."

HHHWWWWWHHHYYYYY did you wait this long?!

My nervous ass started running down the street, trying to make it to the parking garage, while staying on the phone with her to make sure she's ok.

"Teddy calm down, and stop running."

Me, out of breath and panting, "I ain't... I ain't running." Boy, those were the longest three blocks of my life. Once I got to my truck, I hit the highway so hard a toll booth paid ME seventy five cents. I got off the interstate, and Booski texted me saying, "Hurry the hell up!! Get me a red Gatorade, please."

My baby prioritizes.

At the house, she was laying down, fresh out the shower, just having a gang of contractions. I was trying to do the breathing exercises we learned in Lamaze class, but she ain't feeling em AT ALL.
So just tried to make her as comfortable as possible.

While timing the contractions. While telling my stepson and my sixteen-year-old niece to get ready to go to my mom's house. While putting the hospital bag that I procrastinated on HEAVILY together. While her doula was texting me to get her to the hospital ASAP. While tryna keep cool and not piss myself. Bruh. I would go to put the bag together and get dressed and hear, "Oh Teddy, here's another contraction," and have to run back to her so she could put the vice grips on my hand and I could time the contractions. Bruh if I knew she was that damn strong, she would've carried AWWWLLL the groceries when we went shopping.

Next thing I know, the got damn contractions are FOUR... MINUTES... APART!!!

I will not panic.
I will NOT panic.
I WILL NOT PANIC.
EEEEYYYYEE WILL NOT PANIC in front of her.

I called my mom and told her we on the way with the kids, but she gotta be outside waiting, cause that's how strapped for time we were. I was doing a cool 55 mph in a residential area. Hit a crazy ass video game turn into the driveway.

My mother. Lawd my mother. She was standing in the driveway, screaming "YOU NEED TO SLOW DOWN! SLOW THE HELL DOWN!"

I definitely ain't got time to listen to her. So she knocks on the passenger side window to Booski like, "Tell him to slow down!" Booski was slumped over fighting childbirth and ain't even acknowledge my mother. Can't really blame her; she kinda had a baby Jehovah Witness knocking on her cervix.

I got on the highway. Still nervous as hell, but kept it cool on the outside cause she can't be in all this pain and look over at me and see me losing it. I called the hospital and tell em Booski is in labor and we're on the way, and this bullshit happened:

"Ok what's your doctor's name?"
"We're with the Midwives."
"Well you need to call the Midwives."
"Well you need to catch these hands. I ain't yo damn friend. When I come in there cussing with my son crowning through some floral leggings, tell everyone it's your fault!"

They connected me to the Midwives.

Every contraction she had, I gave her my hand to break. Told her how great of a job she's doing. I pulled up to the ER. Got out. Tried to get her out and then…

"OH GOD, I NEED TO PUSH!"

NUH-UH. Check again bruh. I wanted my son to be hard, but not, "born onto concrete" hard. I gave the ultimate pep talk. "Babe you're doing Soooo good. Let's reach deep down and channel the Queen that you are within. Let's focus on these few steps to the ER and I'll be strong for you cause you've been so strong for me. YOU STRONG?! WE STRONG DEN!!!" My baby Boobie Miles'd herself to the ER, crashed in the first wheelchair we saw, and we were OUT to labor and delivery. Got to the room and got her ready. She was on the bed. Rotating, tryna find that spot to deliver. She cocked that left leg up and said "This is it. Let's get it."

Now, I'm squeamish. Like, I get light headed during slasher movies. BUT! This my first child. I had to push that shit to the side, cause I was gonna witness AWL this. The Midwife did something with her finger, and I seen a head fulla hair. The nurse said, "Dad... do you need to step aside and get it together??" *Absolutely!*

"Can we get Dad a chair?" said the genius nurse.

While I was definitely light headed, it was beautiful. I can't explain it, but it was breathtaking. I come back with the A1 gameface and the Midwife told Booski to push. Maaannnn my son slid out like he just integrated the Major Leagues.

I was in awe. Making sure everything was good. Two arms, ten fingers, two legs, ten toes. I just needed to hear my son spit that hot 16 real quick so I could be at peace. Then, he dropped BARS!

I was in love. I gave life. He was so beautiful and perfect. I fell in love all over again with my lady cause we did it. Those nine months were so perfect. I'd do it all over again.

We loved all over him, and the nurse took him, and gave him a shot in his foot and he went Honey Baked Ham. I said, "Get used to it, son. Light skin girls tend to do that to you."

Nurse ain't find that funny.

Josiah "JoJo" Garrick Reid Adams. February 19, 2015. 9 pounds, 5 ounces.

Papa Bear Chronicles

Usually, I'm a reserved guy. I don't pop off in public. Personally, I've never been that offended to show my ass to the world. Once I had a child though, Papa Bear made an appearance. Granted, it took thirteen months, but when he came out, he came out ready for whatever.

I took JoJo to the drug store to pick up some medicine for him cause he had the flu. He was sitting in the cart like a big boy. We were on our way to the pharmacy, playing Patty Cake like some bosses. This taupe kid ran up to the cart. He's about eight or nine, the age of "Know Betterdom," and reached out to touch Jo. I gently pushed the cart back a tad bit out of his reach and said, "Can you say hey, JoJo?" so I wouldn't be 100% rude. The kid just moved closer, so I just had to hit him with the "ightightightightightightightight chill," and started to walk away. Taupe mom goes, "Honey I told you that you have to ask first before touching people's kids. Although that man was very rude."

Time of F*ckedupness, approximately 5:32 p.m.

"Pardon me, ma'am. Am I the rude man you're referring to?" "Yes, my son had good intentions. He loves babies, and you shouldn't have pushed the cart away so rudely." "Did I push the cart away rudely, or did I push the cart away like my one-year-old has the flu? And before I got out my car, I saw BOTH your sons playing bongos on that nasty ass trash can outside before they came in?"

"Well that doesn't-"

"And I'm willing to bet every dollar in my pocket, the three of y'all just waltzed y'all asses in here, you picked up your fruity smelling Shampoo and Soccer Mom Magazine, told them they could each get one snack, and not once made them wash they damn hands. Call me a liar."

Taupe Mom blank stared.

"But I'm supposed to let him rub his hands all on my baby face."

TM, still staring.

"The hand sanitizer is on the counter behind you. Black Lives Matter."

Fade to pharmacy.

Babies & Fools....

Sometime in September of 2014, I got in this crazy car accident. I try not to dwell on it too much. I thank God every day I survived it. I keep the lessons learned with me at all times, but I also keep moving forward. This is what happened though:

I had gotten some GREAT news, so my boys and I linked up to get something to eat and celebrate. I left a little before them to get home and spread the news.

I had always thought I had this texting and driving thing down to a science. Like it'd never happen. God taught me THEE lesson.

I went off the road and went in a ditch. Right when I tried to get out the ditch, I hit someone's driveway like a ramp and my car flipped over twice. I remember AWL of it cause time slowed down.

You know how in movies when it shows a first person angle of someone driving and suddenly, music cuts off, vision is blurry and it's just a bunch of damn noise? Bruh, that's so real.

I knew EXACTLY what I needed to do though. Like I said, when my car started flipping everything slowed down. I said, "Lord, please don't let me die." Soon as my car landed, I needed a second to make sure I was alive and intact. Once I was sure I was all in one piece I jumped out the car and ran.

Why did I run?

Bruh. I'd spent half of my 20's playing Grand Theft Auto, Saints Row, and watching the Fast and Furious series. I ain't finna stand next to no car that just flipped twice that's for dame sure. I was bout to get a few house lengths between me and that car, cause its bout to blow up!

Folk obviously heard me crash so they come outside. I tried to be lowkey. I don't know why. I really don't know why, but for whatever reason, I was standing 25 feet from a flipped car acting like I had no clue what happened or how it got there. A cop pulled up and told me he's surprised I'm conscious. I told him the truth and he asked what insurance I'm with.

"Um.. Farmers maybe? Wait, I just got my insurance card, here you go." "Yea, you must've whacked your head pretty hard. This says Liberty."

Man I just flipped my car I'm not here for real… Green Cross… National Anthem. The Blood. I DON'T KNOW WHAT YOU WANT FROM ME!

My elbow busted the driver side window, so I had to get checked in the ambulance. They gave me the rundown, "I don't see any signs of head trauma, but if your head hurts later go to the hospital blah blah." I needed a nap at this point. I had a bunch of clothes in my trunk in case of a freshness emergency. My trunk wiiiide open, clothes all in the road. It was a whole mess. My phone was blowing up cause my boys left a little after me and took the same way I did and seen my car with my whole wardrobe on display in the street. I ain't answer cause I was looking for moms (yea I'm a mama's boy), but I could only get a hold of my aunt who was at work, but was better at blowing up phones than I am.

I got out the ambulance and see my two 250+ pound homies Timbagland and Rice Cube running towards me. They saw me in one piece and slowed down.

Rice said, "I'm so glad you got out that ambulance. I was running outta breath."

I felt loved.

A dude that I went to high school with lived in one of the houses and came out when he seen me.

"Dude, you ok?"
"I'm ight. I could use some tobacco though."
"Man, look. Take a few of these. Keep the lighter too man, you need all that."

Few minutes later, Mom Dukes, Grandma, and Grandpa pulled up at the scene. I put on the meanest front for my boys. But Mom Dukes could smell BS from a mile away. I fought the meanest urge to let out a struggle cry. Of course, they were just happy the kid was alive and intact.

I took what I could out the car, and the officer told me how sore I'ma be later. "Yea right I ain't no punk. If I was gonna be sore, I'd be sore now."

Bruh. When I tell you I walked around like my knees had concussions. PAIN!!!

All jokes aside, we all think we can text and drive and not end up like folk on TV. I was blessed enough to be here and tell you it's not true. I'm here to show you how REAL GOD IS. I could've died, but luckily I walked out with scratches on my elbow and a bruise from the seat belt. I'm obviously here for a reason. I called this Babies & Fools because that's what God protects. I was obviously a fool, and the good news I was celebrating was the first time I saw my son on ultrasound.

Tip Da Goddess

I love going back home to Raleigh, North Carolina, even if it's for a day, because it's so nostalgic. It's where I call home. So many memories when I cross state line. One memory I have is of an old friend named Tip Da Goddess.

URBAN LEGEND ALERT!!!!

Tip ain't no ordinary female at all. I mean now she is, but she was bout as trill as it came when I first met her. Remember the song Candy Lady by Gucci Mane?? She's the Candy Lady.

I first met Tip Da Goddess when I was 18. Me and my pops were at the Dogghouse in Durham. We frequented the spot, and of course like most Durham hoodgazelles, she worked there. Started casual conversation with her and we later became cool, which brought me deep into the hood circus that she called life. First thing I learned about Tip was that she was ratchet (like most Durhamites) but she was classy, so she was Classchet. She was going to school to teach. But she was also doing dirty work for this rapper who had Durham music on lock. He was known for looking like he was wearing a gold grill from a distance, but as you get closer, you'd see that his teeth were just THAT dirty. He was fittingly known as Stain Gretsky.

She was basically his manager, but she was making little to nothing. Which is why she was working at the Dogghouse, but Stain had some nice hood perks. She got free Nylaters (Now & Laters) at ANY corner store. She got into any club free between 10 and 10:05. AND she got 67% off at Cookout. What hoodgazelle would pass that shit up?

So she'd style this dude in the flyest of hood linens. Set up his performances in Durham Tech's student union, and set up album signings at the Reddest Lobsters in the city! But the wild thing is, she was really doing this shit while going to school full time and maintaining a nice GPA.

Her feyonce, Michael Peeley (light skin dude with eczema), grew up with Stain, but Stain screwed him out of a record deal with Jeans'N'teez Records. See they had been rapping together since high school, and they got attention from the label, but they wanted Peeley more than they wanted Stain. But Stain told the label that it was him who actually wrote and produced everything and Peeley was just a performer. Which was ass backwards so Peeley hates this dude. If he ever found out that Tip was working for Stain, he would've whooped everybody ass, including hers! But he had just joined the military and was out of the state, so she was safe for the time being. Tip had the tuition folk knocking at her door, and Stain was being cheap and the Dogghouse wasn't paying enough. The Ratchet gods must have been calling, cause there was an amateur night at the local strip club. And Tip had BODY. She was hectic bout doing it cause she had morals. She did it, but she didn't take her clothes off cause once again she's Classchet. She just twerked like her rent was on the line. Made three times more than she needed cause the crowd lacked a bountiful amount of electrolytes.

Time went on and Peeley came back and word got out that Tip had been working for Stain and he was PISSED. He demanded that she quit, which she did. Unbeknownst to her, Stain wasn't gonna give her up without a fight.

Stain figured that if Tip was gonna mess with his business, he was gonna hit her where it hurt. He sent his goons out and they jumped Peeley and kidnapped his ass. Told Tip that she'd have to find him cause they hid him in a "super secret place," and if she ain't get there with 10 Gs to fund his "World Tour" around Greensboro, then it'd be a wrap for Peeley.

Luckily for Tip, Stain was an idiot. It took Tip five minutes to realize that Stain had Peeley in his Grandma's kitchen. He got his cosmetology school dropout baby mama scratching Peeley's head, and putting extra strength perm in it, while tapping him on the back of the neck with a hot comb. His goons got the place surrounded. One thing Stain would've known if he had taken the time to get to know Tip was that when she gets mad, she's ratchet Wolverine. Wolverisha.

And although she'd only had a couple minor run ins with the law, she was a criminal mastermind. She knew how to get Peeley back and not get caught.

She took a couple blue popsicles and froze em SUPER HARD. Sliced them into the shape of delicious raspberry flavored shanks. Then ran up in the back door and sliced up anybody that was in the way of her getting Peeley back. I mean blood and corn syrup EVERYWHERE. By the time cops got there, the scene was too damn sticky to investigate so they said, screw it. They ain't like Stain no way.

Tip took the money from Stain's grandma house, and her and Peeley moved somewhere further down South. I'm not gonna tell where she ran to, but she's doing good. Her and Peeley got married and had a couple kids. They both got great jobs and they're enjoying life. I'll tell her y'all asked about her.

5 Finger Manno

URBAN LEGEND ALERT!!!!
The Story of 5 Finger Manno.

So I used to spend some time in Jersey City. There was a girl I was dating, who later became the mother of my child, whose family was all from the city.

I'm out of place when I travel up North, so I have a hard time fitting in. One route I tried to take was bringing up celebrities and such that I knew was from the area since her brothers have been there their whole lives and know a lot of people.

I WILL NOT mention their names, because of the stories they have for them, but at least half of the discussions went like:

"Man you talking bout such and such?!?! Maaannn Five Finger Manno slapped that muhf*cka up in the park!"

EVERY. STORY. Started like that.

Who was Five Finger Manno?! Why was he slapping everybody?? And where is this park I need to avoid so I don't get slapped??? Initially I didn't believe it. But one day, I went to a local bar in the city to partake, and overheard someone else who I didn't know mention someone getting slapped in the park by Five Finger Manno.

I said enough is enough. Time to find out more about this Five Finger Manno. I went looking for his story. And I got it, eventually.

So Five Finger Manno was born and raised in Jersey City. He was very musically inclined, but his favorite instrument was the bongo. As he got older, he developed a short temper. And he couldn't stand nonsense. So he'd be in this park I never found the name of, and him and his boys would play music for fun. If someone looked at him wrong, he would get up and BLAAAOOOOWWW. Just slap fire out of them, just cause HE felt offended. HE felt it was justified. Eventually he made a name for himself. Kinda for his music, but mostly because he was really out here slapping people up in the parks. It was crazy. He became a serial slapper around the city, and folk knew he was coming.

See, he had his bongo strapped around his shoulder as he walked through the city, and he would play a tune on it as he walked around. So when locals heard that bongo, they would scatter. But people from outside the city didn't know, and thought they were getting a free show then, BLAAOOOWWW. What made things worse was that EVERY night and morning, he would work out with hand grips just so folk would fear Five Finger Manno, and tell other towns about him.

Eventually, he became a menace to society, and the police tried to catch him. The thing about Five Finger Manno was that he was light brown with long dreads down his back. Fluent in Spanish and Patois, so folk couldn't describe his nationality. He spoke clear English when he wasn't slap happy. Folks couldn't give a clear description.

There was this one Italian officer who was bullied by dark skin folk while in high school, and he joined the force and made it his mission to terrorize them no matter the age. He hid behind his badge. His name was Blanco Privilegio. Officer Privilegio made it his mission to take down Manno, but he just couldn't. Every time he saw Manno, he would stop and frisk him, but he couldn't nail him cause he was speaking English, didn't have his bongo, and his dreads were tucked tight under a hat that for whatever reason would NOT come off. He would always say, "Manno Ima get ya black ass!" And Manno would resist slapping an officer, cause he knew he would get sent up the river.

One day, Manno was in the park playing, and this guy looked at him funny. It pissed him off so much, he dug deep down in his soul and slapped bruh out of his socks. After the slap he stood over top of him and realized bruh was severely cock eyed. He couldn't help but look at him funny. Everyone in the park banded together and scolded Manno. One lady said, "I'm calling Privlegio."

Manno jumped on the first thing smoking to DC, and hid out for a while. Before he went to sleep, he prayed for help with his anger. He didn't really want to slap people. He just felt it was the only thing necessary in that situation. As he slept, he was visited by an angel, Della Grease. She said, "Manno, you have sooo much aggression inside of you. It could be used for good instead of evil like you've been doing. Until you use this excellent elbow grease for good, I will take one of your glorious dreads. Go against me, you will be Stevie Wonder. Follow me, and you will be Buju Banton. The choice is yours. You will know when it is time." If there was one thing Manno was extremely proud of it was his locks. He had worked so hard on them, and they were responsible for 90% of the girls he bagged. So, he couldn't lose them.

One day, Manno's family was on their way down south to see his little sister and invited him. He figured the further south he went, he would be safe, so he went. Mama Manno's favorite restaurant was Golden Corral. He hated the place, but liked making her happy, so he went. He was eating decent, trying his best to stay upbeat and enjoy his food. The waiter came and refilled his drink, but he reached over his plate to do so.

"I can't believe his rude ass is reaching over my bourbon chicken." Family, in unison, "Manno, please don't do it. "It's cool. It's a good deed."

BLAAAOOOOWWW!!!

Server back-flipped all into the meatloaf. Glasses landed in the green bean casserole. Whole restaurant froze up. Manno confidently smiled.

Then two dreads hit the floor.
He angrily stormed out the restaurant.

"Della Grease, he disrespected me. He got dealt with, why did I lose some locks?!" "Manno, that man is doing his job. Slapping him for a mistake is no good deed."

Manno continued south with his family. Manno made it down south and stopped by a gas station for some backwoods and coconut water. cause you gotta hydrate naturally to fulfill your slap destiny. The cashier didn't hand him his money. He put it on the counter.

"Oh so, I'm not good enough for you to hand me my money?!?!" BLAAAOOOOWWW !!!

Manno slapped this man so hard he caught his whole face. Slammed him against the register and EVERYBODY got $10 free gas. Two more dreads fell out. "Manno, young Manno. You will know when you need to fulfill your Slapstiny."

Manno knew better this time. He didn't argue. Manno stayed down south for a few months with his sister, and didn't go out to refrain from slapping people. His homie had a big show in Jersey City and he figured it had been long enough for the coast to be clear, so he caught a bus up there. While he was waiting for the show, he went outside to smoke. And who else did he see besides Officer Privilegio, roughing up a black teenager who kept screaming, "IM NOT RESISTING MAN! I DONT HAVE ANYTHING!!" Manno was fighting the urge at first, but then he hears Della.

"Manno.... OOOOOOOOHHHHHH MANNNOOOOOO!!! You don't need a watch to know what time it is!!"

"Say no more, Della! Hey PRIVILEGIO!!"

Privilegio let the teen go and ran right towards Manno full speed. Manno grew his four dreads back. Then they all turned Golden. He knew his Slapstiny would be fulfilled. He began to run towards Privilegio, reached his hand up, and came down so hard he had flames coming from his hand. He connected. Privilegio flew back, and hit the side of a Bodega so hard he left an imprint in the bricks that paved the building. The teen fled freely. The rest of the officers rushed to Privilegio's side and are all in shock of what they see. One rookie cop said, "Man he can never work ag-" while his partners hushed his words. Privilegio's partners wept softly for their fallen soldier.

Privlegio regained consciousness in a hospital two weeks later. Surrounded by fellow officers giving him police paraphernalia for all that he had done for the city. "Why are you giving me this?! It's just a small scar I'll be back soon."

Then the Chief said, "No Privilegio. You won't. You can't come back." Privilegio unraveled the bandages from his face and revealed a large hand print shaped scar that has "Black Lives Matter, Ho" on the inside, written in scars. He looked at his comrades distraught knowing it would never heal.

He screamed loudly from his hospital bed "MAAANNNNOOOOOOOOOOOO!!"

Manno smiled as he walked around his old stomping grounds, playing the bongos for onlookers to enjoy.

Hopefully one day I get to meet the new, reformed Five Finger Manno.

The Tale of Bruh Johnnie

I love a good vigilante movie. They're like the black woman of movies. A character sees the law doing a bullshit job of protecting and serving, and they just say, "F*ck it. I'll do it." One of my favorite vigilante stories is one I'm almost certain you've never heard before. So I'm gonna do you guys a favor and get you hip to the greatest story never told.

It's the story of Bruh Johnnie.

Bruh Johnnie was THEE BEST black vigilante right after Nat Turner. Hailing from a tiny town bout the size of a Cadillac Deville by the name of Edgefield, South Carolina. Bruh Johnnie was born in the late 20's to sharecroppers. The oldest of like, 193 children, cause you know black folks ain't have birth control, so they just kept ping ponging babies out like it was nothing.

Bruh Johnnie was born right before the Great Depression hit, so he had to drop out of elementary school to hit the fields and hold it down for his big ass family. Bruh Johnnie was ridiculously strong. I mean like, you need an animal slaughtered, he'd just put it in a sleeper hold and have the body ready to be prepped in two minutes, strong. Needed your field plowed? You ain't need any oxen. Just strap a plow to his ass and promise him some pigs feet later, and your field would have the freshest lineup you could imagine. To go along with this strength, Bruh Johnnie was the best fighter in Edgefield. Ironically, he wasn't a violent man. The only time he fought was if someone in his family or a woman was disrespected. However, over time, he beat every ass that needed it, so no one in the town who knew better would mess with him.

Sometime later, some taupe folk came to town and started wreaking havoc on Edgefield. Taupe folk that liked to wear pointed white hoods. Led by a man named Obediah Lynchisass. Lynchisass was a powerful sheriff and soon-to-be politician that had the law in that town under his thumb. He could get away with practically anything he wanted to.

One day, while Lynchisass' posse was going crazy, Bruh Johnnie decided to fight back. He knew it was damn near impossible to fight an organization that large unarmed, so my man Bruh Johnnie got his Samson on and grabbed a hogjaw (didn't have an ass to de-jaw), and got some big corn cobs for projectiles and went on a spree. Being a sharecropper's son, he couldn't afford a fly costume. Bruh just got an old potato sack and wrote "Bruh J" on it. So here he was, out here fighting racism in Edgefield, South Carolina with the potato sack vest, no mask, and just a driving cap with the brim tilted LOW(so you couldn't see his face) that would miraculously stay on. And of course his suspenders. No matter where you went, you had to wear suspenders in the 30's. Bruh Johnnie hit that red clay running and took out anyone who Bull sent out to jump stupid. He even had a signature call that let you know Bruh was on his way,

"SAAAAAYYYYYY WWHHHHAAAAAAAAAAATTTTT?!!!!!!"

And by the time he was done screaming, you was on ya ass or on the way down. Bruh was that fast.

Of course like any hero, Bruh had his " Bruhisms," you know, things he would say after he saved folk. Like, "Be careful where ya set shit down, cause niggas'll steal ya stuff no soon as it hit da ground." Or, "Don't let ya right hand know what ya left hand doin." And,"Don't let ya britches hang low, cause ya never know if a nigga will try n catcha." Also, "Don't cut the fool out in public." Bruh was a deep man.

This one particular story that I remember being told was when bruh found out that Obediah Lynchisass had sent some of his BITs (Bigots in Training) to go to the playground and rough up Bruh's two youngest siblings, Freddy Thuglass and Soburner Troof. Once Lynchisass messed with Bruh's family, he f*cked up royally. Bruh snuck into Lynchisass's office, locked himself in, and broke his hogjaw over Lynchisass' head in one swing. Then proceeded to unleash a fury of haymakers until Obediah shat himself. Bruh was THAT furious.

Lynchisass' henchmen had heard his screams and were trying to get into his office but Bruh told em.

"You come own in heah, and I'ma knock this fools nuts in the sand PERMANENTLY."

Bruh told Lynchisass that he'd let him live if he promised him one thing, a way for him and his 192 siblings along with his parents to get out of Edgefield for good, or if they chose to stay, to be left alone. Lynchisass, wanting to live, and seeing that Bruh had foam running from his mouth, obliged.

He gave Bruh an hour to get everything together and get out of town. Once that hour passed, he would send his henchmen out to look for him and him only. Lynchisass thought it would be impossible for Bruh Johnnie to pack his whole life up and skip town. Little did he know, Bruh Johnnie was POE and a man of little needs. Bruh was out of Edgefield in twenty five minutes.

He joined the army to send his family some steady money, and then settled down in DC, driving a taxi cab. Fighting the urge to bust heads, all the while wishing a MF would.

This is a true story. I think. I'm not 100% sure. My Grandfather doesn't say much about his past.